Avant-Garde Art

COLLIER BOOKS/ART NEWS SERIES

Each of the anthologies in the series
explores the range of our history from
specific points of view of major importance
to all the arts.

AVANT-GARDE ART
ACADEMIC ART

Avant-Garde Art

edited by
Thomas B. Hess
and John Ashbery

COLLIER BOOKS/ART NEWS SERIES

COLLIER-MACMILLAN LTD., LONDON

The Macmillan Company
866 Third Avenue, New York, N.Y. 10022
Collier-Macmillan Canada Ltd., Toronto, Ontario

First Collier Books Edition

This Collier Books Edition was selected from Art News and Art News Annual XXXIV.

Printed in the United States of America

Contents

Contents

Avant-Garde Art

The Invention
of the Avant-Garde:
France, 1830-80

by Linda Nochlin

Linda Nochlin is professor of art history at Vassar
and also teaches at Columbia. She is the author of
Realism and Tradition in Art and *Impressionism and
Post-Impressionism*, both recently published by
Prentice-Hall.

"Art changes only through strong convictions, convictions strong enough to change society at the same time." So proclaimed Théophile Thoré, *quarante-huitard* critic, admirer of Théodore Rousseau, Millet and Courbet, art historian who discovered Vermeer and one of the spokesmen for a new, more democratic art, in 1855, in exile from Louis Napoleon's Imperial France. Whether or not one agrees with the correctness of Thoré's assertion, it is certainly typical in its equation of revolutionary art and revolutionary politics of progressive thought in the visual arts at the middle of the nineteenth century. Seven years earlier, in the euphoric days following the 1848 Revolution, a new dawn for art

The Invention of the Avant-Garde: France, 1830–80
had been seriously predicated upon the progressive
ideals of the February uprising. At that time the
most important art journal of France, *l'Artiste*, in its
issue of March 12, 1848, extolled the "genius of
liberty" which had revived "the eternal flames of
art" (obviously it had been less effective in reviving
the rhetorical power of its writers), and the next
week, Clément de Ris, writing in the same periodical, while slightly chagrined by the mediocrity of
the first "liberated" Salon, nevertheless maintained
that "in the realm of art, as in that of morals, social
thought and politics, barriers are falling and the
horizon expanding." Even Théophile Gautier, certainly not an apostle of radicalism either in art or
politics, took the opportunity to sing a hymn of
praise to the new era in the pages of the same
periodical. The ages of Pericles, Leo X or Louis XIV
were nothing, he maintained, compared to the
present epoch. "Can a great, free people do less for
art than an Attic village, a pope or a king?" The
question, obviously, is rhetorical.

Delacroix was generally the painter to whom
progressive critics looked for a fulfillment of the
revolutionary ideals of the 1848 uprising; as early
as March, Thoré, in *Le Constitutionnel*, expressed
the hope that Delacroix would paint *L'Egalité sur
les barricades de février* as a pendant to his allegory
of the revolutionary ideals of 1830, *Liberty at the
Barricades*, which had been taken out of storage and
placed on exhibition following the February uprising. Both Daumier and Millet entered the revolu-

tionary government's contest for a representation of the Republic, while Courbet, who toyed with this idea, also seriously considered taking part in the national competition for a popular song.

The very term "avant-garde" was first used figuratively to designate radical or advanced activity in both the artistic and social realms. It was in this sense that it was first employed by the French Utopian Socialist, Henri de Saint-Simon, in the third decade of the nineteenth century, when he designated artists, scientists and industrialists as the elite leadership of the new social order:

It is we artists who will serve you as avant-garde (Saint-Simon has his artist proclaim, in an imaginary dialogue between the latter and a scientist) . . . the power of the arts is in fact most immediate and most rapid: when we wish to spread new ideas among men, we inscribe them on marble or on canvas . . . What a magnificent destiny for the arts is that of exercising a positive power over society, a true priestly function, and of marching forcefully in the van of all the intellectual faculties . . . ![1]

The priority of the radical revolutionary implication of the term "avant-garde" rather than the purely esthetic one more usually applied in the twentieth century, and the relation of this political meaning to the artistic subsidiary one, is again made emphatically clear in this passage by the Fourierist art critic and theorist, Laverdant, in his *De la mission de l'art et du rôle des artistes* of 1845:

Art, the expression of society, manifests, in its highest soaring, the most advanced social tendencies; it is the forerunner and the revealer. Therefore to know whether art worthily fulfills its proper mission as initiator, whether the artist is truly of the avant-garde, one must know where Humanity is going, know what the destiny of the human race is . . .[2]

César Daly, editor of the *Revue générale de l'architecture*, used a similar military term "*éclaireur*" or "scout" in the 1840s, when he said that the journal must "fulfill an active mission of 'scouting the path of the future,'" a mission both socially and artistically advanced.[3] Baudelaire, after a brief flirtation with radical politics in 1848—he had actually fought on the barricades and shortly after, in 1851, had written a eulogistic introduction to the collected *Chants et Chansons* of the left-wing worker-poet Pierre Dupont, condemning the "puerile utopia of the art-for-art's sake school," praising the "popular convictions" and "love of humanity" expressed in the poet's pastoral, political and socialistic songs[4]— later mocked the politico-military implications of the term "avant-garde" in *Mon coeur mis à nu*, written in 1862–64.[5]

Certainly the painter who best embodies the dual implications—both artistically and politically progressive—of the original usage of the term "avant-garde" is Gustave Courbet and his militantly radical Realism. "Realism," Courbet declared flatly, "is democracy in art." He saw his destiny as a continuous vanguard action against the forces of academicism in art and conservatism in society. His summarizing masterpiece, *The Painter's Studio*, is, as we shall see, a crucial statement of the most progressive political views in the most advanced formal and iconographic terms available in the middle of the nineteenth century.

Courbet quite naturally expected the radical artist to be at war with the ruling forces of society and at times quite overtly, belligerently, and with obvious relish challenged the Establishment to a head-on confrontation.[6] The idea of the artist as an outcast from society, rejected and misunderstood by a philistine, bourgeois social order was of course not a novelty by the middle of the nineteenth century. The advanced, independent artist as a martyr of society was a standard fixture of Romantic hagiography, apotheosized in Vigny's *Chatterton*, and he had been immortalized on canvas by at least two obscure artists by the middle of the nineteenth century; both of these paintings serve to remind us that there is no necessary connection between advanced social or political ideas and pictorial adventurousness. The sculptor Antoine Etex's unfortunate *Death of a Misunderstood Man of Genius*, (now in Lyons, one of the many crosses which French provincial museums seem destined to bear), was deservedly castigated by Baudelaire in his *Salon of 1845*, and is an obvious and derivative reference both to Chatterton and the dead Christ or Christian martyr. Somewhat more successful, because more concrete and straightforward, is an English variation

The Invention of the Avant-Garde: France, 1830–80
on the theme of the artist as a social martyr, Henry
Wallis' *Death of Chatterton*, an overtly sentimental
and marvelously detailed costume piece, praised by
Ruskin in his 1856 *Academy Notes* as "faultless and
wonderful."[7]

It is not until seven years after the 1848 Revolution that the advanced social ideals of the mid-
nineteenth century are given expression in appro-
priately advanced pictorial and iconographic form,
in Courbet's *The Painter's Studio*. Its truly innovating qualities are perhaps best revealed by comparison with the "revolutionary" painting of the
uprising of 1830, Delacroix's *Liberty at the Barricades*, a work conservative in both the political and
the esthetic sense, that is to say, nostalgically Bona-
partist in its ideology and heavily dependent upon
mythological prototypes by Delacroix's Neo-
Classical teacher, Guérin, for its iconography and
composition.[8] On the other side of the political
fence, democratic and humanitarian passions seem
to have been no more a guarantee of pictorial
originality in the case of the Revolution of 1830 than
they were to be in that of 1848. Although he was far
more politically radical than Delacroix, Philippe-
Auguste Jeanron's *The Little Patriots: A Souvenir
of July, 1830*, which appeared in the 1831 Salon, is
obviously a watered-down, sugar-coated re-working
of Delacroix's romantic, molochistic allegory, *Greece
Expiring on the Ruins of Missolonghi*, which had
been exhibited at the Musée Colbert in Paris in 1829
and 1830. Jeanron, a close friend of Thoré, was later

8

named director of the National Museums under the 1848 Revolutionary Government, and he accomplished miracles of reorganization and democratization during his brief incumbency. Yet, as is so often the case, good intentions are no guarantee of innovating, or even memorable, imagery. Despite contemporary and localizing references in *The Little Patriots* such as the dome of the Panthéon (?) in the background or the paving stone barricade to the left, the pall of the academic *poncif* hangs heavier over the painting than the smoke of revolutionary fervor; one is made all too aware, in the pose of the little patriot in the center—reminiscent of that of Donatello's *David*, and so appropriate in its iconographic implications—that Jeanron was an art historian as well as an artist.

Certainly, there had been no dearth of paintings with socially significant, reformist or even programatically socialist themes in the years between the Revolution of 1830 and that of 1848. In 1835, Gleyre planned a three-part painting to be titled *The Past, the Present and the Future,* represented by, respectively, a king and a priest signing a pact of alliance; a bourgeois, idly stretched on a divan, receiving the produce of his fields and his factories; and The People receiving the revenues of all the nation. In the Salon of 1837, Bézard exhibited a social allegory, rather transparently titled *The Race of the Wicked Rules over the Earth,* and in the 1843 Salon, the versatile (or perhaps eclectic) Papety exhibited his controversial *Dream of Happiness* now

The Invention of the Avant-Garde: France, 1830–80
in the Musée de Compiègne. In 1845, Victor Robert
exhibited *Religion, Philosophy, the Sciences and the
Arts Enlightening Europe*, while in 1846, no less a
figure than Baudelaire himself deigned to notice the
Universal Charity of Laemlein, a bizarre confection
representing a personification of Charity holding in
her arms three children: "one is of the white race,
the other red, the third black; a fourth child, a little
Chinese, typifying the yellow race, walks by her
side."[9] Works such as these of course lent themselves perfectly to satire: both Musset and Balzac
made fun of the ambitions of the apocalyptic and
Fourierist painters, probably basing their caricatures on that learned and mystical pasticheur of
universal panaceas, Paul-Joseph Chenavard.[10]

Yet one of these allegorical, socially progressive
artists working prior to 1848 is worth examining
more closely, if only to lend higher relief to the
truly advanced qualities of Courbet's post-revolutionary *Studio:* this is the little-known Dominique
Papety (1815–49), for a time one of Chenavard's
assistants, dismissed by Baudelaire in his 1846
Salon under the rubric "On Some Doubters," as
"serious-minded and full of great goodwill," hence,
"deserving of pity."[11] What is interesting about
Papety is that he was a Fourierist, and Courbet's
Studio is among other things a Fourierist as well as
a Realist allegory. Yet in the difference in conception, composition and attitude between Papety's
allegory and that of Courbet lies the enormous gap
between painting which is advanced in subject but

conventional in every other way and that which is truly of its time, or even in advance of it (to use the term "avant-garde" in its most literal sense) and hence, a pictorial paradigm of the most adventurous attitudes of its era. Papety's Fourierist convictions were stated in a language so banal that his *Rêve de Bonheur*, although Fourierist in inspiration, looks almost exactly like Ingres' apolitical *Golden Age* or Puvis de Chavannes' *Bois Sacré*; the elements identifying it with contemporary social thought are completely extraneous to the basic composition. While a critic of 1843 saw "a club, a people's bank or a phalanstery" in "this dream of the gardens of Academe," and noted the unusual amalgamation of Horace's *Odes* and Plato's dialogues with the steamship and the telegraph, the expendability of these contemporary elements is revealed when *L'Artiste* announces that Papety, on the basis of critical advice, has replaced his steamboat with a Greek temple, "which," remarks the anonymous critic, with unconscious irony, "is perhaps more ordinary but also more severe than socialism in painting."[12]

The link—and the gap—between Courbet and Papety is most clearly revealed by comparing the *Studio* with Papety's ambitious plan for a truly doctrinaire Fourierist painting, *The Last Evening of Slavery*, executed about 1848 for a fellow Harmonian, François Sabatier, of Montpellier, a friend and supporter of Courbet and a close associate of the latter's patron, Alfred Bruyas, himself an apostle of the New (Fourierist) Harmony. Courbet's *Studio* may be seen in part as a translation into contemporary, concrete, personal terms of the Fourierist generalizations written in red letters beneath the sketch itself of Papety's grandiose but never completed project. Courbet doubtless had become familiar with Papety's sketch during the course of his visit of 1854 to Bruyas, an eccentric who envisioned himself as a "salesman of the New Harmony" and actually went so far as to publish an abortive Fourierist tract, *Notes d'Harmonie*.[13] During the summer of 1854 Courbet visited Sabatier on his estate at Tour de Farges near Montpellier where he drew Sabatier's portrait in black pencil. Sabatier, while highly appreciative of Papety's works, had already written a eulogistic account of Courbet's *Burial at Ornans* and *Peasants of Flagey* in his *Salon of 1851*, praising their truthfulness, dignity and democratic spirit. Sabatier, poet, linguist, translator, knowledgeable amateur of music and the theater, was married to Caroline Ungher, one of the great singers of the epoch. A warm friend of the arts, he was also deeply concerned with the lot of the poor and the humble; as a partisan supporter of the 1848 Revolution he was forced to flee Paris during the terrible days of June, when the forces of reaction took their revenge. He practiced the doctrines of Fourierist "Association" mainly by his support and encouragement of artists such as Eugène Devéria, Chenavard, Hébert and, above all, Papety. On his family estate, he cultivated his vineyards or drew up plans for phalansteries. No doubt, the ambitious sketch executed by Papety was at least in part suggested to him by his Harmonian patron, who in turn showed the drawing to Courbet and discussed the ideas embodied in it with him. Courbet himself was certainly a staunch partisan of socialist thought, partly because of his close association with the anarchist revolutionary, P. J. Proudhon, who had himself been deeply influenced by Fourier as a young man and had supervised the printing of one of Fourier's books. More specifically, in his fragmentary autobiography of 1866 Courbet notes that by 1840 he had left behind his youthful training in order to follow socialists of all sects, and that "once arrived in Paris, he was a Fourierist."[14] In 1850, he had made a drawing of the Fourierist missionary Jean Journet going off to spread the gospel of Universal Harmony. In a sense then one might say that Papety's mediocre and pedantic drawing offered Courbet a challenge: whether he could translate Papety's academic classicism into a pictorial language of his own time derived from his personal experience.

Art historians have always been hard-pressed to explain both the inspiration and specific implications of Courbet's *Studio*. It seems to me that a Fourierist interpretation, in conjunction with Papety's drawing, while it in no sense completely "explains" Courbet's allegory, at least helps to elucidate some of its otherwise inexplicable aspects: for example, just why Courbet chose to include the figures he did in his vast composition. Papety's sketch stipulates the depiction of "Scholars who have made the hour of Harmony [the final stage of Fourierist evolution] advance" and "Artists and poets swept up by enthusiasm [a specifically Fourierist term]"; the entire right-hand side of Courbet's painting consists of artists, philosophers and thinkers, who, in his opinion, have played an important role in the formulation of the new world. Papety mentions a "great strong man"; Courbet depicts a doughty athlete. Papety specifies a crowd of workers; Courbet, with greater economy, gives us a laborer and his wife. Papety mentions a "sick, worn-out worker"; Courbet has depicted "a poor, weather-beaten old man" in his left-hand group. Papety presents religious figures in a derogatory light; for Courbet, the rabbi and the priest in the *Studio* are personifications of self-satisfaction and hypocrisy. Papety had planned to represent "an aristocratic group surveying the scene"; Courbet placed two elegantly dressed visitors or spectators in the foreground. The Harmonian Leader, who was to have occupied the center of Papety's composition, is of course Courbet himself, the artist, busily engaged in creating a landscape in the center of his painting.

Even aside from the specific analogies between Courbet's canvas and Papety's drawing, further elements link the *Studio* with Fourierist conceptions: for example, the Fourierist ideal of the Association of Capital, of Labor and of Talent is clearly embodied in Courbet's iconographic scheme. Fourier's system depends on a series of complex correspondences among the natural, the physical, the psychological and the social realms. For example, the Four Affective Passions, cornerstones of the Fourierist system—Friendship, Love, Ambition and Family Feeling—correspond to the four ages of life: Childhood, Adolescence, Maturity and Old Age, all embodied by figures in Courbet's painting. Yet there is actually a fifth stage, to be inserted between that of adolescence 16 to 35) and that of maturity (46 to 65 years), a phase which, according to Fourier, does not count in this system since it is the pivot, and the pivot never counts in the calculation of movement. That is the phase of virility, from 36 to 45 years, to which correspond the Affective Passions of both Love *and* Ambition—in other words, the plenitude of life. Now interestingly enough Courbet reached his thirty-six birthday in 1855, the year of the Universal Exposition for which the *Studio* had been planned and in which it was completed; Courbet is indeed, quite literally, the pivot of the painting, the immovable center around which all pictorial activity takes place; in addition he is flanked by an adoring nude muse (Love?) and is looked up to by an equally admiring little boy (Ambition?). The cat, incidentally, was one of Fourier's favorite animals, although the presence of the elegant and eminently paintable animal in the foreground can hardly be accounted for in terms of doctrine.

One of the most puzzling minor sidelights of

Courbet's composition is the significance of the little boy scribbling a picture, a later insertion whose presence has been accounted for both as a mere space-filler—to balance the still-life objects on the left-hand side—and as a personification of the newly-awakened interest in the art of children associated with the Swiss, Rodolphe Töpffer.[15] Yet here again a Fourierist interpretation best accounts for this figure. Fourier was extraordinarily interested in the nature and development of children and in formulating an appropriate pedagogical system designed to take advantage of their innate inclinations and at the same time foster the well-being of the phalanstery as a whole. One of the five major dispositions of children observed by Fourier, and one of the ones most worthy of cultivation in his opinion, was *"la singerie"* or *"the mania for imitation."* Children, according to Fourier, should have their own little tools, their own small-scaled workshops, where, under the tutelage of their elders, their natural imitative propensities might best be put to productive ends. Surely the little boy diligently working away on his crude drawing is learning through imitation; initiated by a masterpainter, he himself will become one of the masters of the future.

Yet still another question remains to be answered about the mysterious and provocative iconography of the *Studio*. If François Sabatier was indeed a crucial figure in the conception of the painting both as a follower of Fourier and as the owner of the

Papety sketch which provided at least partial inspiration for Courbet's masterpiece, why is Sabatier not represented in the work itself, as are such other crucial figures in Courbet's career and thought as Champfleury, Bruyas, Baudelaire and Proudhon? It is my contention that Sabatier is indeed present, although only partially; he may well be the half-hidden husband of the elegantly-dressed woman in the foreground: the wealthy patron come to survey the scene. Certainly the line of hair and beard and the little tuft of hair that protrudes on the forehead are similar to these features in the black pencil drawing in the Musée Fabre in Montpellier. Further investigation would of course be necessary to establish the identity of the elegant wife in her flowered shawl with Caroline Ungher Sabatier and that of the man who accompanies her with other securely identified portraits of Sabatier. Nevertheless, even without such assurance the identification is a tempting one.

Courbet's painting is "avant-garde" if we understand the expression, in terms of its etymological derivation, as implying a union of the socially and the artistically progressive. Far from being an abstract treatise on the latest social ideas, it is a concrete emblem of what the making of art and the nature of society are to the Realist artist. It is through Courbet, the specific artist, the Harmonian demiurge, that all the figures partake of the life of this pictorial world, and all are related to his direct experience; they are not traditional, juiceless abstractions like Truth or Immortality, nor are they generalized platitudes like the Spirit of Electricity or the Nike of the Telegraph; it is, on the contrary, their concreteness which gives them credibility and conviction as tropes in a "real allegory," as Courbet subtitled the work, and which, in addition, ties them indissolubly to a particular moment in history.

While one might well reply that Ingres' *Apotheosis of Homer* is as irrevocably bound to the same historical moment as Courbet's *Studio*, even though it attempts to establish universal values and eternal verities, in the case of Ingres' work, this is *despite* rather than *because* of the intentions of the artist; one might almost say that as far as Ingres was concerned, to be of one's time was a measure of failure rather than of achievement. By the middle of the nineteenth century the distinction between the contemporary and the avant-garde has already begun to make itself felt. Ingres' painting is, of course, in no sense "advanced"; it merely smells of its epoch to trained art-historical nostrils, as does all art.

Yet if we take "avant-garde" out of its quotation marks, we must come to the conclusion that what is generally implied by the term begins with Manet rather than Courbet. For implicit—and perhaps even central—to our understanding of avant-gardism is the concept of alienation—psychic, social, ontological—utterly foreign to Courbet's approach to art and to life. While Courbet may have begun his career as a rebel and ended it as an exile, he was never an alienated man, that is, in conflict with himself internally or distanced from his true social situation externally, as were such near-contemporaries as Flaubert, Baudelaire and Manet. For them, their very existence as members of the bourgeoisie was problematic, isolating them not merely from existing social and artistic institutions but creating deeply felt internal dichotomies as well.

In other words, their birth into the middle class was a source of internal as well as external alienation. Such a situation would have been utterly foreign to Courbet, who proudly accepted and even exaggerated his provincial petty-bourgeois background into something overtly plebian and rustic, emphasizing his regional *patois* and the simplicity and directness, if not outright coarseness, of his manner.

With Manet, the situation becomes far more complicated. For the first time, we are confronted with an *oeuvre* which, like the dandy himself (who was originally postulated as the human equivalent of a work of art), lives completely autonomously, as gratuitous and non-communicative as Baudelaire's frigid incarnation of Beauty. How can one possibly take Manet at his word—and does he, in fact, wish us to?—when, in the catalogue statement for his private exhibition of 1867, he assures us that it is merely the "sincerity" of his works that give them their "character of protest," or when he pretends to be shocked at the hostility with which the public has greeted them. "Manet has never wished to protest. It is rather against him who did not expect it that people have protested. . . ." These words ring hollow in the face of such outright affronts to public sensibility as *Déjeuner sur l'Herbe* or *Olympia*. What has never been sufficiently taken into account by "serious" criticism is the character of these works as monumental and ironic put-ons, *blagues*, favorite form of destructive wit of the period, inflated to gigantic dimensions—pictorial versions of those endemic pranks which threatened to destroy all serious values, to profane and vulgarize the most sacred verities of the times. Significantly enough Manet, greatly at ease with "popular" turns of phrase, employs the term *"blague"* at least six times in the course of his (rather brief) recorded pronouncements.[16] The Goncourt brothers devote a rich and rhetorical paragraph in *Manette Salomon* to a discussion of the *Blague*:

The farcical *Credo* of scepticism, the Parisian revolt of disillusionment, the light and boyish formula of blasphemy, the great modern form, impious and charivaresque, of universal doubt and national pyrrhonism; the *blague* of the nineteenth century, that great destroyer, that great revolutionary, that poisoner of faith, killer of respect. . . .[17]

No wonder, then, that an outraged critic, no worse than most, exclaimed before *Le Bain*, as the *Déjeuner* was known in 1863: "This is a young man's practical joke." And indeed, the *Déjeuner sur l'Herbe*, with Manet's brother, brother-in-law-to-be and favorite model, Victorine, staring blandly out of the décor of Giorgione's venerated pastoral idyll, their elegant contemporary costume —or lack of it—making a mockery of the "timeless" Raphaelesque composition, must have seemed as full of protest and constituted as destructive and vicious a gesture as that of Marcel Duchamp when he painted a mustache on the Mona Lisa.

For Manet and for the avant-garde, as opposed to the men of 1848, the relation of the artist to society was a phenomenological rather than a social fact. He was involved in both the society and the political events of his time—his project for the mural decoration of the new Hôtel de Ville in Paris, with its series of compositions representing *"Le Ventre de Paris"* of 1879, his paintings of *The Execution of Maximilian* and *The Escape of Rochefort*, as well as his activities during the seige of Paris and the Commune, bear witness both to his involvement and to his desire for accuracy of reportage. But Manet's works can hardly be considered direct statements of a specific viewpoint or position. Quite often they seem more like embodiments of his own essential feeling of alienation from the society of his times, a dandyish coolness toward immediate experience, mitigated either by art or by irony, or his own inimitable combination of both. The most authentic statement of Manet's sense of his situation as a man and as an artist may well be his two versions, painted in 1881, of *The Escape of Rochefort*, in my opinion unconscious or disguised self-images, where the equivocal radical leader, hardly an outright hero by any standards, is represented in complete isolation from nature and his fellow men: he is, in fact, not even recognizably present in either of the paintings of his escape from New Caledonia. It is no longer a question of the Romantic hero in the storm-tossed boat; there is no ideological or physical contrast between controlled serenity and natural passion in Manet's paintings as there is in their prototype, Delacroix's *Christ on the Sea of Galilee.* And even here, it must be noted, the faintest ghost of *blague* enters into the tone of the painting, with its open, ultra-Impressionist brushwork, its invisible protagonist and the vague, Chaplinesque figure at the rudder. The isolation here is built into the imagery, as it is in Manet's whimsical single stalk of asparagus, his lone rose, his centralized pickle-jar: it is not the result of the observation of a specific social situation, it is an artful and pathetic statement of how it is to be an artist, how it is simply to be in the world at all.

This vision of isolation receives its apotheosis in *The Bar at the Folies-Bergère,* perhaps the most poignant image of alienation ever painted, a deadly serious spoof of Watteau's *Gilles* in completely modern "naturalist" terms, the anonymous yet concrete figure trapped between the world of tangible things and that of impalpable reflections, existing only as a way-station between life and art. It is upon just such bad faith and alienation and the marvelously inventive, destructive and self-destructive ways of making art about them that the modern avant-garde has built ever since. This is far indeed from Courbet's unified and unselfconscious vision of art and society—and his own direct and unambiguous relation to both—in the 1855 *Studio of the Artist: A Real Allegory of Seven Years of My Life as an Artist.*

1. Henri de Saint-Simon, *Opinions littéraires, philosophiques et industrielles*, Paris, 1825, cited in Donald D. Egbert, "The Idea of 'Avant-garde' in Art and Politics," *The American Historical Review*, 73, No. 2, December, 1967, 343.

2. Cited by Renato Poggioli, *The Theory of the Avant-garde*, trans. Gerald Fitzgerald, Cambridge, Mass., 1968, 9.

3. Cited by Peter Collins, *Changing Ideals in Modern Architecture: 1750–1950*, London, 1965, 261-62.

4. "Pierre Dupont," originally published 1851, Baudelaire, *Oeuvres complètes*, ed. Y.-G. Le Dantec and C. Pichois, Paris, 1961, 605, 612, 614.

5. Poggioli, *op. cit.*, 10.

6. See, for example, his deliberately provocative behavior toward the Comte de Nieuwerkerke, Director-General of the Imperial Museums, and his activities related to the Vendôme column incident during the Commune.

7. *Collected Works*, ed. E. T. Cook and A. Wedderburn, London, 1902–12, XIV, 60. The painting is now in the Tate Gallery.

8. See Pierre Gaudibert's extremely interesting analysis of Delacroix's essential conservatism, "Eugène Delacroix et le romantism révolutionnaire: A Propos de *La Liberté sur les Barricades*," *Europe*, 41, April, 1963, 4-21. For Guérin's influence on the *Liberty*, see Sixten Ringbom, "Guérin, Delacroix and 'The Liberty,'" *Burlington Magazine*, 110, 1968, 270-74.

9. For the best source of information about these socially-conscious painters prior to 1848, see Léon Rosenthal, *Du*

The Invention of the Avant-Garde: France, 1830–80
romantisme au réalisme, Paris, 1914, 345-98. Also, Joseph
C. Sloane, *French Painting between the Past and the Present*,
Princeton, 1951, passim.

10. For a complete account of this fascinating failure, see
Joseph C. Sloane, *Paul Marc Joseph Chenavard*, Chapel Hill,
1962.

11. "Salon of 1846," *Art in Paris: 1845–1862*, ed. and
trans. J. Mayne, London, 1965, 101.

12. *L'Artiste*, June 2, 1844, 80.

13. For information on Bruyas and Sabatier see Montpellier, Musée Fabre, *Dessins de la collection Alfred Bruyas*,
1962, introd. Jean Claparède, n.p. (Inventaire des Collec-
tions Publiques Françaises, 6).

14. "Biographie de Courbet par lui-même," in P. Courthion, ed., *Courbet raconté par lui-même et par ses amis*,
Geneva, 1950, II, 27.

15. Meyer Schapiro first made this connection between
Courbet's little boy and the Swiss artist Rodolphe Töpffer's
ideas about the art of children, "Courbet and Popular
Imagery," *Warburg Journal*, 4, 1941, 178 and n.4.

16. *Manet raconté par lui-même et par ses amis*, ed. P.
Courthion, Geneva, 1945, 27, 28, 30, 162, and passim.

Gustave Courbet: *The Studio* (detail), 1855. Louvre, Paris.

Claude Monet: *The River*, 1868, 31⅞ inches high. Art Institute of Chicago.

Claude Monet: *Westminster Bridge*, 1871, 18½ inches high. Collection of Lord Astor of Hever, London.

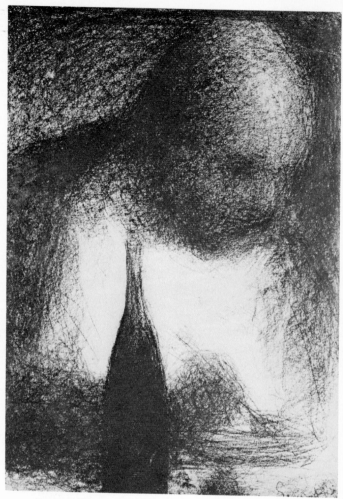

Georges Seurat: *Man Dining* (the artist's father), ca. 1883, conté crayon, 12½ inches high. Art Institute of Chicago.

Louis Anquetin: *Butcher Shop, Place Clichy, by Night,*
1887, 27 inches high. Private collection.

Gustave Courbet: *The Studio* (detail), 1855. Louvre, Paris.

Gustave Courbet: *François Sabotier,* 1854.

Jacob Epstein: *Female Figure*, 1913, flenite, 24 inches high. Minneapolis Institute of Art.

Monet, or the World Turned Upside-Down

by Michel Butor

Ever since Michel Butor's *La Modification* won the Prix Renaudot in 1957, he has been looked upon as one of France's leading novelists and, together with Alain Robbe-Grillet, the principal exponent of the objective style of the *Nouveau Roman*. Though known in this country chiefly for his fiction, he is also a brilliant poet and essayist, with a special concern for art.

THE TRANSIENT

FIDELITY to nature is the crux of the Impressionist strategy against the Salon or the Academy, yet one should observe the paradox introduced into it by Claude Monet. When Courbet or the young Monet says that he paints objects or people *as they are*, he implies that this may be verified; for these painters, the model must have a certain stability, must stay put, so that their representation may be compared to it, point by point. It must, therefore, be a tranquil landscape, a still-life, a ceremony, a moment of leisure. The fact of painting outdoors or with broad strokes changes nothing in these fundamental truths: indeed, one may verify the exactness of nuance as, in the Renaissance, that of detail. But Monet, with his insistence on the transient, destroyed the old fidelity. The traditional verification became impossible, denied not only to the spectator but to the painter himself. The colors he put on his canvas no longer corresponded to those he saw. The delineation of reflected light had obviously changed.

Nor should one say of him "What an eye!," as Cézanne did, but "What a memory!" He portrayed the transient so truly that we are forced to conclude that he painted in the absence of his subject. The composition is as complete as in the Franche-Comté landscapes that Courbet reconstituted in his studio. But in Courbet, as later in Cézanne, such reconstitution is based on something permanent, at the viewer's disposition, whereas in Monet it is based on something which, by definition, has disappeared forever. Our only means of verification is the encounter in nature, during a walk, of an *effect* of the same kind, having the same kind of difference from habitual vision. The instantaneity of Monet, far from being passive, requires an unusual power of generalization, of abstraction. Corot's and Courbet's *realist* landscapes said: here is nature, not as painters ordinarily represent it, but as you see it yourselves. Monet declares: here is nature, not as you or I habitually see it, but as you are able to see it, not in this or that particular effect, but in others like it. The vision I propose to you is superior; my painting will change your reality.

It was therefore necessary for him to discover unstable objects, subjects that contain a dynamism which can intervene in the viewer's vision.

Compare his landscapes with those of Sisley. Sisley adopted everything in the art of the young Monet that may be taken as a continuation of the art of Corot, but Monet's instability remains foreign to him. In Sisley all is calm. In the dark apartments of Paris or London, he opens windows giving onto a countryside or a peaceful suburb, airy, luminous, where time slows down. One feels that nothing has moved from the time he set up his easel to the time he finished the painting. In *The Flood at Port-Marly*, he spreads before our eyes the surface of a perfectly calm stretch of water reflecting light, making colors fresher; the reflections are there only to let us know that it is water; they have no interest in themselves. In Monet, on the contrary, the reflection as it was, now forever gone, is often the heart of the composition.

PORTRAIT OF MME. GAUDIBERT

With Monet one is no longer calmly regarding nature, or the exterior, from within; instead, this exterior sets about invading the room in which the painting is hung. When he rambles through the fields or forests, "like a hunter," what he is looking for is not something that lends itself to painting but, as he wrote so often in his letters, something "impossible to paint," something that will allow him

to give the final surface of his painting that dynamic
instability which is the essential of his art.

One of the simplest ways of doing this would
seem to be to paint a figure in motion, like Degas
or Lautrec. But Monet was quick to reject this
solution. For the immobilized creature remains
immobilized in its frame. Monet is closer to his goal
when he can achieve an immobility which is ending,
for then the immobility of the work is justified: a
movement for us will be the result.

At the Jeu de Paume in 1964 two very important
works, done at nearly the same time, hung side by
side: the *Portrait of Mme. Gaudibert,* and Manet's
The Balcony. At this point, Monet was still learning
from the older painter, yet a detail common to both
works reveals a fundamental difference. In *The
Balcony,* Jenny Claus is putting on her gloves. Mme.
Gaudibert is also putting on her gloves. They have
reached almost the same stage. But in *The Balcony,*
there is no sense of urgency. One feels that Berthe
Morisot, in the foreground, might remain there for
hours while behind her, in the shadows, servants
softly came and went. Jenny Claus is turning her
hands in utter tranquility. It is a long drawn-out
moment which the painter prolongs still further. He
develops its leisure. Mme. Gaudibert, however, is a
study in nervousness; it is as though the pose exas-
perated her. The fact of not being able to see the
artist who was painting her, turned away as she was,
must have irritated her throughout the sittings; she
is waiting only for permission to turn away com-

pletely and flee. Her tall figure is immobilized but straining toward the viewer. Eventually all her dress will whirl, rustling.

THE RIVER

In the *Portrait of Mme. Gaudibert*, everything except the lady is immobile. How to brighten the surface, how to make the painting invade the room where it hangs? To do this, Monet sought forms that necessitate a perceptual reorganization in ourselves. The simplest diagram, characteristic of his art, absent from that of his friends, is reversal: the act of turning an object upside-down.

When we see a house with its roof at the bottom, we still think of the roof as on top, and consequently animate the image; we will be continually putting it right side up, and continually finding it upside-down. If everything is upside-down, the painting itself is upside-down and need only be adjusted; for animation to be permanent, inverted images must be combined with normal images.

The River is Monet's first authoritative resolution of this problem.

A young woman, probably Camille Monet, is seated on a grassy bank, in the shade of a tree. At her right a rowboat is moored; across the water there are bright houses. A Corot, one would say. But the woman's face is a single blotch, neither detailed nor individualized in any way, so as not to hold our attention. What does attract it is the re-

31

flection, under the tree, of houses which we don't see, hidden by the foliage, upside-down houses fully as bright and precise as the ones we see directly, and whose forms are distorted slightly by ripples coming from the boat.

The role of the woman's face is to center the symmetry. The houses to her right have the roof above, those to her left have it at the bottom. This arrangement forces us to reestablish, behind the foliage, the reflected houses' normal image, registered on the water's broken surface to the left as a completely reversed reflection of the other houses. The whole painting comes alive in these divisions.

IMPRESSION—SUNRISE

In *The River*, certain parts of the painting give us a precise account of what is going on in another part, of something hidden or momentarily interrupted. We no longer see an object, but rather its decomposing original. We reassemble and scatter the fragments of the image indefinitely and thereby restore its movement to the water.

This is evident in the famous *Impression—Sunrise*, which gave the Impressionists their name. The red circle in the upper part is there to tell us that the complex stripe of the lower part is the sun's reflection which we would certainly not suspect if the painting were cut in two. The upper half is a title for the lower.

From the moment the identification is made, the

whole surface comes alive in waves, the original circle dissolves and reforms according to a definite rhythm. Furthermore, the vertical length of the reflection brings the light toward us, near us; we are bathed in its rays.

As for the name that Monet gave this work, it is its necessary complement: it emphasizes his composition while adding a new element to it. It has already been noted, in fact, that if one considers the picture by itself one cannot tell whether it depicts a morning or an evening; the mention, "rising sun," lends the red circle an ascending movement and so emphasizes this advent of light.

REGATTAS AT ARGENTEUIL

If we isolate the lower right-hand quarter of the *Regattas*, 1872, and reverse it, we have a painting of remarkable color intensity, violently drawn, a Fauve work. All the elements composing it, which might otherwise be slightly obscure, are explained by the upper half, which says: this is a boat, this is a house, etc. The reflections incite an analysis of what is enumerated above.

It is as if Monet were saying to us: you do not know how to see this red and this green, so beautiful in their pure state, but look: they are in this house.

It is impossible to interpret the reflected part as the simple notation of what lay before the painter's eyes. How can one suppose that Monet would have chosen any one of the millions of images that a

33

camera might have registered? He constructed an image, animated by a certain rhythm, which we may imagine as conforming to that of the liquid surface (yet there is nothing to confirm even this), based on real objects.

The semantic relation of above and below obviously works in both directions: a) the upper names the lower: this aggregate of blotches which means nothing to you is a tree, a house, a boat; b) the lower reveals the upper: this boat, this house which seem dull to you contain secret congruences of color, elementary images, expressive possibilities.

The upper part corresponds to what one recognizes, the reality one is used to; the lower, which leads us toward these houses and boats, corresponds to the painter's act. The water becomes a metaphor for painting. The very broad strokes with which these reflections are indicated are vigorous assertions of material and means. The liquid surface provides us with an instance in nature of the painter's activity.

MME. MONET IN JAPANESE COSTUME

The canvas is a surface which the eye develops in depth. Monet, during his *hunts*, looked for objects whose surfaces give a direct impression of thickness.

This thick surface is the key to this extraordinary work in which even Monet, toward the end of his life, hesitated to move with certainty.

It was his wish, he states, to use a red hanging, but he was intrigued by a length of silk decorated with extraordinary thick embroideries, representing a furious samurai unsheathing his sword. The result was this strange composition of a dancer with head bent back, fanning herself, before a wall decorated with a scattering of round fans.

Camille's face is painted without emphasis, hardly indicated; the heart of the work is the head of the samurai, whose volume is much more clearly drawn, grimacing on her hip; here we have what amounts to a still-life. The symbolism might inspire a psycho-analyst, but we will limit ourselves to noting the structural ambiguity governed by the two faces; the real and the false face, the latter more vivid than the former.

Despite their hostility, some early critics were aware of a characteristic element: the fans scattered on the wall seem to come together in a dance around the woman, as though suspended in air and con-nected with her gesture. Except for the stripes below, there is no perspective; the distance to the wall remains vague, and because the details of the fans are treated more minutely than the face of the woman, they tend to advance almost as far forward as the head of the samurai.

We shall soon observe a double deception in Monet's painting: a) the deception common to all painting of illusionary space which we are obliged to read as landscape or interior; b) the deception which comes from the apparent thickness of the painted surface itself, making an embroidery as startling as that of a Japanese robe.

Just as there is a pulsation in the surface between the upright and reversed images, there is a perpendicular pulsation between the apparent thickness of the painting and the thickness of its subject.

WESTMINSTER BRIDGE

Such movement in depth, which gives Monet's work its aggressiveness, is possible only through breaking the rules of traditional perspective.

In fact, when a precise scenography assigns to each element its exact distance, the space depicted, with its irregularities, its real or apparent thicknesses, will become so much stronger than the painting's surface that the latter will be completely forgotten. Leaning as it were on the handrail of the frame, the spectator will allow his imagination to wander in the distance, disappearing down the roads of Ruysdael, hovering over the Arcadias of Claude Lorrain.

Monet cuts this flight short.

Usually he does it by choosing a subject whose plane is similar to a painting's: a steep bank—say Argenteuil, Vétheuil, Carrières-Saint-Denis, etc.— seen from the other side of the water. The plane of the water, horizontal in nature, representing the act of painting itself which brings the distant object to us, will always seem to be in the process of becoming vertical, like the canvas.

In such an arrangement the problems of perspective, provided one foreshortens some lines and roof angles, do not arise. At times, however, Monet likes to bring into his painting lines that are perpendicular to it and that would ordinarily *flee* toward the vanishing point, with the risk of thereby halting all interpretation at a definitively fixed distance, thus depriving the work of its dynamic forward motion, its provocation. Ruysdael, Claude Lorrain and even Corot base their work on this *flight*; it is essential to them. But each time that conventional perspective occurs in his image, Monet neutralizes it. In one of his first views of London, *Westminster Bridge*, the Abbey is developed parallel to the canvas as in the famous subsequent paintings, but the wharf on the right constitutes a perspective cluster that might well form an optical trap. Monet offsets it, first by the construction of horizontal and vertical black girders whose presence is much more striking than the wharf's, and above all by contriving a counter-cluster, disguised as floating sticks that in nature would constantly change places, adding the motif of instability.

THE SEINE AT BOUGIVAL AND THE PORT AT ARGENTEUIL

Hobbema's *The Avenue, Middelharnis* at the National Gallery, London, is well known. The double row of slender trees emphasizes the perspective, so that the "flight" into the picture becomes vertiginous. The spectator is a prisoner of its void. In Monet's work there are often rows of trees perpendicular to the painting, but their effect is very different, since Monet employs an illumination parallel to the picture plane, in which the trees cut out sections of light and shadow. Thus they appear as poles between which sheets of light and dark are strung, and the vertical planes they define become more important than they.

The house-fronts of Vétheuil or Argenteuil become curtains of light and darkness, and the liquid surfaces, the metaphorical water, begin to permeate the entire work.

As against the deep, vertiginous space of Dutch painting, Monet's space overflows toward the spectator. It is as if the surface were constantly producing first a white wave, then a black wave, then a white wave.

UNLOADING COAL

Unloading Coal is a crucial example of these vertical, parallel planes in action. The barges and wharves, perpendicular to the painting, ordinarily would induce a steep "flight," but Monet counteracts it with the bridge in the upper part and especially by all the narrow intersecting gangplanks on which the dockhands are coming and going, with their extraordinary hats, which lends the scene a sort of Far-East picturesqueness.

The different parallel planes by which space is

divided are no longer only those of light and shade, but of movement in either direction, of heaviness or lightness. The shadow hardens into charcoal-black; the rhythm of the waves given off by the painting is no longer that of water or walking, but that of effort and relaxation; it is the exact rhythm of heavy labor, imposed by the artist on the spectator.

The aggressiveness of nature reminding the citizen that it exists is here joined to the claims of the workingman, whose movements are thrust on the rich man's consciousness. The initial exoticism of gilded color, hats, etc., emphasizes the violence of this intrusion.

The Railroad Bridge at Argenteuil

In Dutch painting the void created by perspective stressed the solidity of the objects, the merchandise displayed by merchants, and then, in the greatest painters, derided materialism and invited the viewer to another life. In Monet it is the space itself that presents a plenum, that causes an upheaval among the objects, gnaws them, destroys or transforms them. Their atmosphere is no longer an exquisite calm, but takes on such presence that it fills the space of the room.

This accounts for the fundamental role of the wind in Monet's art; it is the means by which the intervals between the objects represented will no longer be voids but centers of pressure and activity.

39

Monet, or the World Turned Upside-Down

The wind blows in Ruysdael, too, but it takes us toward other shores, it is an invitation to voyage; in Monet, it blows toward us, sustaining the emanation of the surface, thrusting apart neighboring objects.

A dress lifting, a scarf fluttering, the handle of a parasol firmly gripped against the wind, the curvature of sails are like so many arrows, endowing space with tension. Later, noise will be added.

The Railroad Bridge at Argenteuil assembles the broken surface of water, the rhythm of light and dark planes suggested by the columns, the powerful arrow of the chugging train, with the noise we associate with it, in the opposite direction from its smoke which the wind blows back toward us.

A little later, the series on the Gare St. Lazare develops the theme of trains, their noise and smoke, in very different ways. The rhythm of arrivals and departures, of crowds delivered and taken away, the pulsation added to the life of the city, are all dealt with.

RUE MONTORGUEIL DECKED OUT WITH FLAGS

There are other noises than those of trains, shouts for instance, which may be recorded in writing. Monet indulged himself once only, I believe, in such an experiment. The canyon of the street is filled with flags and the wind that waves them. Among these tricolor streamers, carefully opposed to the movement of the whole, a pennant is unfurled with

40

the inscription "VIVE LA FRANCE." One does not always notice it at first; often it must be pointed out to the viewer before he sees it. But suddenly it strikes the eye, as a cry would strike the ear. Once one's attention has been drawn to this phrase, one discovers that it is repeated in gold-yellow on the white part of one of the foreground flags. Thus the cry is heard and fades away.

THE BREAK-UP OF THE ICE

Waves, wind and noise, led Monet to search not only for thick surfaces, but thickening surfaces, which are themselves emanations.

The water, troubled as it may be, must remain smooth to offer reflections. Freezing is an important mode of its thickening. The river will be covered with a rough crust; but then it will reflect nothing, it will be petrified.

Between these extremes, of the mirror with no substance of its own, pure reflection, and the rugged ice on which images no longer form, the whole metaphor of painting comes into play; whence the theme of *The Break-Up of the Ice*, when the crust dissolves to reveal upside-down fragments of the trees on its banks.

If one considers water as matter, it has these characteristics: a peculiar transparency that may be evidenced by algae, such as the purplish trailers of *Boating on the River Epte* (São Paulo Museum); when sufficiently ruffled, it will rise in drops of spray, in foam, mist, all these phenomena accompanied by odors and noises whose recollection will come back to us precisely insofar as the painter manages to retain the dynamism of its thick surface. Sometimes the emanation of the water becomes fog, invading the entire painting and, as is well known, bringing objects closer together, as in the great London series.

The Wild Poppies and The Poppy Field Near Giverny

The Wild Poppies (Musée du Jeu de Paume) is a typical early example of the thick, dynamic surface: we sense that the grass in the field is moved by the wind, so clearly indicated by the flying scarves of the two women. How did he manage to rid those red splotches of their fixity, how is it that they do not seem to be attached to the ground?

There is a disproportion of scale here: seen close-up, these corollas that grow smaller and closer together the farther away they are from us, are much too big in relation to the heads of the women, or the children. It is a double scale that allows a double surface: the flowers wave at us above and at the end of their slender stems.

This disproportion became one of Monet's favorite techniques: the characteristic detail considerably magnified in relation to the surface it defines. Thus a comparison of *The Cliff at Etretat* at the Clark Art Institute, Williamstown, Mass., and the photograph taken by William Seitz of the same site makes stunningly obvious Monet's exaggeration of the striae of the chalk. In just this way, the grasses of the field have gigantic blades and the straws of hayricks are the size of small logs.

In the Boston *Poppy Field* the red and green spots that melt into a dark brown in the distance are in no way imitations of the forms of the flowers and leaves but, as we necessarily interpret the red as being the color of the petals and the green as that of the background, they give the impression of seeing the red in front of the green. They are at first complements, then two colors interacting in the foreground, melting away in the distance to a third, very different shade, the union of these two colors or, more exactly, of this red overlay and the green depth peculiar to it, becoming a real development.

ROUEN CATHEDRAL

The disappearance of orthodox composition, noted in the Boston *Poppy Field*, will eventually give the work a real power to repel. The manner of the young Monet, remarkable, so lively, various, disappears for a while in a clogged surface in which his individuality drowns. This is especially evident in the Cathedral series, whose principle is the development, in an indefinite number of works, of that duplication which we have seen in the *Regattas at Argenteuil* and so many other paintings. Each version, then, can be for any other version what the upper part was for the lower: the reciprocal animation of surfaces is thus carried to its limit.

In the Cathedral series, nearly all the paintings show the façade from the side; some, however, show it from the front but they do not form a separate group. This is because the side perspective of the majority is counteracted by the absolute unity of the paint-matter, and by the fact that the near is not characterized by more detail than the far.

Close up, line and brush-stroke dissolve to such an extent that one cannot tell where stone ends and sky begins. One has the impression of standing before the cement wall of a building which has just been destroyed or put up, an indecently exposed surface without its usual paint or wallpaper.

The surface of the canvas betrays the surface of the wall on which it's hung and which, in general, it helps to mask.

What attracted Monet initially to the façade of the cathedral at Rouen was its remarkable thickness, its hollowed, bristling quality; what held his interest was the fact that such visual properties came to the support of an interpretation in which everything it represents comes into play.

It is a sacred object that invades the worldly apartment. The cathedral is cut off in such a way that it leaps from the upper right-hand part of the canvas, indefinitely prolonging itself; and, in the side views, it produces a sort of banging shutter effect, since the oblique angle vanishes as soon as one goes closer, to reappear when one stands back.

The solid matter, the wall, no longer a *represented matter*, which is a very different deception, can be found again in the subject, in the cathedral itself, if we go and see it, if we move in close. Between the known object and the denatured painting, this house-painter's painting which echoes it, all the usual stages of viewing will be contained. At a certain distance the impression of *painting* will dominate; a little farther away, or a little later, appears the matter of the surface of the façade, the hollowed, bristling effect, a texture very different from what we are used to in masonry; it is this matter from which will emanate all sorts of imaginary matters, rustling gold, spurting silver, the sky descending.

Monet recognized in the architect of the cathedral at Rouen an intention comparable to his own; he too had achieved a surface by means of which a revelation might be produced, in the ordinary as well as the most religious sense of the word: a surface to bring the sky into the center of the city, let it in, to make it sink in the earth: a sky seen as gold, or lightning, or blackness, or ice.

THE WATER LILIES

A similar intention may be observed in *The Water Lilies*, a monument to peace produced in the midst

Monet, or the World Turned Upside-Down
of World War I. Far from fastening on an effect
glimpsed during a walk or "hunt," Monet diverted
the course of the river Epte to form a special little
backwater. The work *from nature* is still quite perceptible in the beginning of the series, done in 1898;
in the late painting at the Orangerie, all traces of it
are gone.

Monet was almost blind by then. He suffered
from a double cataract and a disturbed color-per-
ception. In some astonishing paintings, done just
before his operation, the hues are entirely *invented*.
Even after recovering the use of his eyes, he could
no longer trust them; always working with num-
bered tubes, he went on what he knew about
pigments rather than on his *impressions*.

The Water Lilies of the Orangerie is a completely
constructed work; the real pond in it is no longer
there as model (or alibi), but as a *key*. Here is what
the painter says: "If I remained unaware of the
subtleties and modulations of color seen close up,
I was yet able, standing at a distance, to contem-
plate the blocked-out theme; and this was the point
of departure for new themes. To be honest, a very
modest point of departure. Cautious, I wished to
leave nothing to chance. I slowly set about testing
my capacities in countless sketches which convinced
me that the study of living light was definitely impossible for me, but also reassured me, even while
proving that my little games of tone and delicately
tinted landscape were over, that my eye was as

sharp as ever for vivid colors isolated in a mask of dark.

"What use could I make of this?

"My intentions formed slowly. I had always had the idea, since my sixtieth year, of applying myself, in each thematic category that had successively pre-occupied me, to a kind of 'synthesis' in which I would sum up, in one or perhaps two canvases, my past impressions and sensations. I had discarded this idea. It would have been necessary to travel often and far, to see again, one by one, all the places of my life, to go through old emotions. It occurred to me, in doing my sketches, that a series of coherent impressions, taken down at those times when my sight was likeliest to be clear, would not be without interest. I waited for the idea to take shape, for the ordering and composition of the themes to slowly inscribe themselves on my mind, and for the day when I felt readiest to take my chances, with some hope of success. So, I made up my mind to act, and I did."

Cosa Mentale

With this composition already in mind, Monet had no idea of setting up his easel before the pond to reproduce it, but instead sent for a contractor to build him a new studio: "Walls with no opening except the door; the ceiling to be two-thirds sky-light." The war prevented its construction, but the

47

painter achieved an equivalent in his old studio, having easels on wheels constructed, which allowed him to be entirely surrounded by the work in progress.

The water in *The Water Lilies* must have saved his eyesight. As distant as he had remained all his life from the classical myths, here he finds them in his title (*Nymphéas*), spelt hundreds of times by the flowers; he is invoking the goddesses of the fountain.

No longer able to trust color, he came to define the painting's elements by a vocabulary of brush strokes. In this sense, *The Water Lilies* is a recapitulation of his whole œuvre, but on a monumental scale. He worked on oppositions of calculated hues, whose properties he had already tested. All those details which would formerly have escaped him to figure as *fleeting effects*, now submit to the over-all composition.

Great cilia of reeds or river-line rushes, vertical downy trunks, little vertical cilia of willow leaves, clogged surfaces of upside-down clouds, horizontal, of varying length, more or less trembling on the water's surface, great enveloping strokes for the water-lily leaves and dazzling blotches for their flowers.

The lifting of the horizon, already so perceptible in earlier paintings, is now absolute; the sky and distance no longer appear except upside-down, and the water's surface tilts toward the vertical, inducing a dream of flight or of diving.

Some of the trees repel by the falseness of their woolly substance—one feels they are painted as *décor*, or meant to be seen from a distance farther than is possible at the Orangerie. The surface of the water comes toward us imperturbably from a distance impossible to define. The perspective set up between the flowers remains uncertain, if only because of the curving wall. But any repulsion is balanced by the enclosing welcome of the whole liquid, elliptical expanse coming at us from all sides, making the trees slip behind us in an incessant movement.

Thus we slowly fall into the sky; the waters of the sky fall on us.

Monet has retained only a few traces of the usual landscape: the water absorbs them, animates them, reveals a thousand-and-one properties in them. The canvas is a thick mirror of germination; the lilies make everything intelligible.

In the real pond of Giverny, the look of the world would have been reflected, even without flowers; but in the painting its figuration appears only by virtue of their presence. They are the nymphs of the springs, who have entered the city to oblige us to turn ourselves upside-down.

Translated from the French by Lane Dunlop

The Neo-Impressionist Avant-Garde

by Françoise Nora

Françoise Nora is a young French art historian
with a special interest in Neo-Impressionism. She wrote
her dissertation on Signac and edited his writings.
She is attached to the Department of Paintings
at the Louvre.

THEIR *succès de scandale* at the Salon of 1874 left the Impressionists feeling more hurt than proud. They had been trying to get accepted, to show that they were right, to prove that their painting was true and beautiful, truer and more beautiful than that of the academic establishment and, though modern, nonetheless in the great tradition of Flemish and Venetian art. Their temperaments were naturally happy, except as material vicissitudes affected them, and they wished to give painting back its vitality and its special power to communicate an immediate sensibility through the eye and the hand to the outside world.

(This does not of course apply to Cézanne, who was more profoundly revolutionary and pleased to shock the public.)

Barely a decade later the attitude of a certain number of emerging young painters was totally different. Their consciousness of who they were, of their obligations and aims, was infinitely further removed from the Impressionists than the latter had been from the Barbizon School. With the Neo-Impressionists we are dealing with painters who, for the first time in history, believed they had advanced beyond their predecessors and made this "progress" the very essence of their theory. And around 1885, as at the time of the first wave of Symbolism, there was a kind of contamination of political ideas which became to a certain extent sublimated in the arts. Less than 15 years after the Commune and the re-establishment of bourgeois order, the collective consciousness of young intellectuals was permeated with nostalgia for revolutionary purity, as well as a sadness and an exigency which can be analyzed at length in poetry as in painting. There is in Seurat, for instance, something of an esthetic Saint-Just.

At the very moment when writers were discovering a "Mission to get rid of old-fashioned ideas" (*Le Décadent*, June, 1886), Seurat was constructing on canvas a mathematical utopia, an austere and ideal order. This was the period of full-blown Positivist euphoria, of certitudes, of the triumph of science and history. Darwin's theory of evolution had become a general conviction in the '80s, and had profoundly changed people's consciousness of the time they lived in. They now knew that they were in the midst of evolution, and they wanted it to be progress. For the first time, writers (the Symbolists) and painters believed and desired to be in the avant-garde—a state of mind which was to spread rapidly during the years after 1886 among artists whose aims were far removed from those of the Neo-Impressionists. But it is highly significant to grasp that this key-idea so essential to our contemporary art arose with the Neo-Impressionists, whose goal was to reconcile art and science.

The notion of the avant-garde replaced, around 1885, that of modernity. The Impressionists, painters of the modern in Baudelaire's sense of the word, were against academic painting. The Neo-Impressionists, on the other hand, no longer even cared about official art and the Salon, but they opposed the most modern painting of their time, that of Monet and Renoir. To wish oneself avant-garde presupposes, in a way, a revolution which has begun, an army already on the march. It involves a radicalism which may at any moment become obsolete, "outflanked on the left," and is therefore a very fragile concept.

Seurat has often been taken to task for his hypersensitivity, his concern to point out on every occasion that he was the first to create optical painting. The history of twentieth-century art has accustomed us since then to these quarrels over priority, but this one seems to be the first of its kind, like the one the same year between Gustave Kahn and Marie Krysinska over the origin of "free verse." For the first time the artist lays claim to a date at the same time that he invents—fascinating testimony not only to Seurat's consciousness of the role he was playing in the evolution of art history, but also to his confidence in his technique. Thus he dreaded, somewhat naïvely, to see it divulged, and stressed its novelty as its most precious element: "The more of us there are, the less original we will be, and the day when everybody will be using this technique, it will have no more value and we shall have to seek again—which is already happening. It is my right to think this and say it, since I painted this way in order to find something new, a painting that would be my own," Seurat wrote to Signac in 1888. He was perhaps first to incarnate not only the avant-garde, but also what one might call "avant-gardism," the feverish anxiety which it presupposes and which we find so often in the art of today. His remark seems to be a reply to an article which appeared in *La Justice* and which was typical of what was being said less than three years after *La Grande Jatte*: "Seurat's and Signac's marine scenes and Dubois-Pillet's barges are already only the middle ground of Independence: they are left-of-center and perfectly correct. And now Anquetin inaugurates his *cloisonnisme*. Will yesterday's revolutionaries resign themselves to becoming classic, stereotyped, old hat?"

Jacob Epstein: *The Rock Drill*, 1913-14. Tate Gallery, London.

Wyndham Lewis: *Woman's Head,* 1911, drawing.

David Bomberg: *In the Hold,* 1913-14, 78 inches high.
Tate Gallery, London.

Carl Andre: *Scatter Piece*, 1967, plastic and canvas bag. Dwan Gallery, New York.

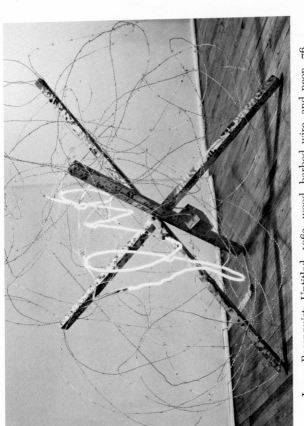

James Rosenquist: Untitled, 1963, wood, barbed wire, and neon, 76 inches high. Castelli Gallery, New York.

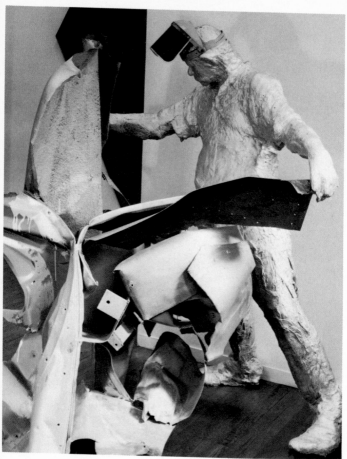

George Segal: *John Chamberlain Working*, 1965-66 (Chamberlain car-metal sculpture and Segal's plastic figure of Chamberlain). Collection of William S. Rubin.

Boccioni: *Elasticity*, 1912. R. Jucker, Milan

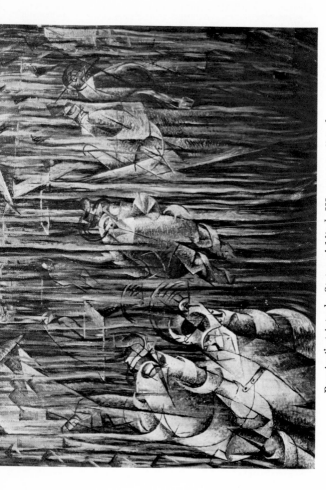

Boccioni's triptych: *States of Mind, III*, 1911, 27¾ inches high. Private collection. New York.

Anquetin's Cloisonnism, which Gauguin was soon to transform into a style, is something of a premonition of the stages which Henri Matisse, successively influenced by Seurat and Gauguin, was to pass through in 1905. But for the moment, in 1886, we are in the happy days of Symbolism, whose scientism nourished Seurat's thinking. For the Neo-Impressionists the science of color and their discontinuous technique—stemming from the need to reconstitute from a distance a color and a shape previously broken up into their basic elements—were the sign of a universal harmonic key to nature, a desire for unity. What we have here, confused and merely implicit, are old pre-Socratic notions revived by recent discoveries about the structure of matter. Wasn't a critic (Teodor de Wyzewa) saying at that very moment of Mallarmé: "All is symbol, every molecule is big with the universe, every image is the microcosm of all nature"? Through their technique, Seurat and Signac, like the Symbolist poets, no longer wished to express visible nature, but eternal nature; no longer the "rudimentary states" Valery speaks of, but a second reality, the intimate structure of things. Fénéon understood this from the beginning, when he defined, in his delectable and precious decadent prose, the ambitions of Neo-Impressionist art, which "sacrifices anecdote to arabesque, nomenclature to synthesis, the transient to the permanent and, having grown somewhat weary of nature's precarious reality, confers on it an authentic reality."

The idea of the avant-garde at the end of the century was closely linked, in all the arts, with nostalgia for a remote past. Delacroix and the Impressionists annexed Holland or Venice; each describes a certain modernity. The Post-Impressionists —Seurat, van Gogh, Gauguin—have their eyes fixed on the future, but at the same time aspire to the purity and the grandeur of vanished styles. Gauguin's and Seurat's methods are in a certain sense parallel: Gauguin dreamed of linking up with what he thought of as the grand opera of the golden age as he was preparing the style of tomorrow—pictorial liberty and what he himself called "the right to dare everything"; while Seurat wished to be the Giotto of the age of science and to paint universal harmony as it emanated from its organic laws. As were Rood, Helmholtz and Charles Henry for the modulations of technique, it appears that Charles Blanc was, more than any other, the intellectual master of the first Neo-Impressionists. He had formulated the optimistic program to which Seurat and Signac, formed by his *Grammaire des Arts du Dessin*, were to subscribe: "Thus humanity, guided by a star which is the memory of its past grandeur and the hope of its future grandeur, will march toward the conquest of Paradise Lost, that is to say of the true, the good and the beautiful, and it will recapture these forms of happiness through science, industry and art. Science will dissipate errors; industry will conquer matter, art will discover Beauty." Plato in the engine-room! This double movement which consists in simultaneously preparing the future and salvaging a distant, ideal past is significant for all the political and intellectual avant-gardes, and stems from the Hegelian and Fourierist ideologies with which Charles Blanc, the old *"quarante-huitard,"* was imbued.

The underlying humanitarianism of Charles Blanc's works did not have the same implications for everybody. For Seurat the revolution is one of artistic technology, but in the Neo-Impressionist group of the heroic period, when the ideology was being formed which after 1890 was to attract van de Velde, van Rysselberghe and Finch for varying periods of time and to allow H. E. Cross to realize himself, Seurat had, with regard to the concepts of the avant-garde and progress, an attitude different from those of Signac, Pissarro, Luce or Angrand. In the minds of the latter, to be avant-garde was to be political as well as esthetic, and it was their attitude which characterized the movement for their contemporaries, as much as the novelty of the style. Jules Christophe associates the two ideas naturally when, à propos of Seurat, he recalls the revolutions of 1848 and of 1871: "The Commune in art was proclaimed by a young man of 27" and when he calls Pissarro "The Blanqui of the brush." But Seurat never took a definite political stance; on the contrary everything seems to indicate that his aristocratic individualism turned him away from political commitment.

In contrast, Pissarro and especially Signac read Reclus and Kropotkin, the theoretician of anarchy; they were associated with Jean Grave, the leader of the libertarian movement, and Jules Vallès. Maximilien Luce, the only painter of the group of working-class origin (Seurat and Signac came of bourgeois—even typically bourgeois—families), and Felix Fénéon, their art critic, were soon to be so closely allied with the anarchist movement that they were arrested and imprisoned in 1894 after the criminal attempts of Ravachol and Henry. A few years later, the Dreyfus affair, which split French society in two, found the Neo-Impressionists without exception on the side of the Dreyfusards (which was not at all the case with the Impressionists), and in the 1914 war they were pacifists.

It is idle to speculate how, in painting as in his opinions, Seurat would have evolved if he had not died at the early age of 32 in 1891. But around 1886 what immediately stands out in the work of Seurat and his friends, besides their common technique, is their choice of subjects and their vision of the external world. They painted the most desolate aspects of the suburbs, industrial landscapes, workers bathing, in a spirit completely different from that of Monet, even when he painted the Gare Saint-Lazare. Their representation of the petty-bourgeois world of Paris is steeped in irony. The bourgeois boredom, immobility and niggardliness depicted in Seurat's *La Grande Jatte* reappear in Signac's *Sunday*, without at any point constituting a genre scene.

The Impressionist world is prosperous, its meadows are luxuriant, its nudes opulent, its crowds given over to earthly joys. What Neo-Impressionism evokes, around 1886, is a world that is waiting, empty, where something is going to happen, where one holds one's breath: whence the sadness and mystery of the least bit of wall or pier or beach in Seurat and Signac. It is a vision of nature that is radically new in relation to a classical vision; it situates the real in a distance of alienation.

This de-realization is one of the most revolutionary elements of the technique. The yoke of the system of small brushstrokes, of optical mixing and of the science of the relationships of lines has paradoxically resulted in a liberating element: an escape toward pure painting. The spectacle of the world and the skill of the painter, filtered through a Symbolist scientism, made of the canvas itself a mathematical object, a domain of research which no longer has much to do with the world of appearances. The surface of the painting reflects only itself. One can see the consequences that such an attitude would have for Cubism and abstraction.

After the death of Seurat, Neo-Impressionism is Signac and Cross, for whom the revolution and the avant-garde were placed under the sign of color: all of their painted and written work bears witness to it. But in 1886, when the movement was truly avant-garde, the theme of both scientific and poetic research seems to me to be that of light. In 1887 when Pissarro was a fanatical divisionist enrolled under the banner of Seurat he wrote to his son Lucien about the advances which Neo-Impressionism had made over Monet, "the romantic Impressionist"; he stressed the fact that Monet paints "dark" and that Renoir seems "black." Paul Alexis uses the same terminology for Seurat: "It is impossible to achieve greater light with greater harmony." This obsession with luminosity seems laden with both scientistic and symbolic implications. Light, clarity, the spark are images which occur repeatedly in the traditional revolutionary vocabulary. As for Seurat's crayon drawings, their extraordinary newness resides in the fact that for the first time drawing is not attached to an outline but totally dissolves it in the interests of a single effect: light looming out of darkness.

This obsession with light might seem nothing more than a poetical transcription of the temper of the '80s, whether it be *Liberty Lighting the World* (Bartholdi's statue dates from the same year as *La Grande Jatte*) or the industrial use of electricity, at that time the symbol of human progress. Seurat in fact wished to name his movement "Chromo-Lumin-airist" but was obliged to accept the term chosen by Fénéon in homage to Pissarro, the aging Impressionist and recent convert to the new sensibility.

But in Seurat, light has a highly personal, affective resonance and a particular sublimation. Let us leave the last word to him (in a letter to Signac of July, 1886): "Then what more is there to say? Indeed that's enough for today; time to go and get drunk on light once more: that is consolation."

The New Constructive Geometric Art in London, 1910-15

by William C. Lipke

William C. Lipke, assistant professor of the history of art at Cornell University, specializes in twentieth-century Britain. He has recently completed a book on David Bomberg, published by A. S. Barnes.

Avant-garde British painting of 1910–15 parallels the satellite movements in Russia and Germany which clustered about the theories and pictorial devices of Cubism and Futurism. Yet Vorticism and the new constructive geometric art —as manifested in the work of Wyndham Lewis and David Bomberg—go beyond the derivations of the Rayonnists or German Expressionists when confronted with the Cubist and Futurist experience. What then is the relationship of avant-garde British painting of the pre-war era to that of Italy and France?

Cubism and Futurism gave the British artists an impetus to break with the past and also provided an esthetic and an approach which was immensely significant for the development of Vorticism and the new constructive geometric art. Part of the impact of Cubism on the work of Wyndham Lewis and his coterie has been noted by John Berger:

Certain original stylistic features of Cubism can be found in the pioneer works of other movements: Suprematism, Constructivism, Futurism, Vorticism and, later, the de Stijl Movement and Dadaism.[1]

These influential "stylistic features" were essentially: 1) a compositional device and an ordering motif that was reductive in nature—what Berger has referred to as the use of the *diagram*;[2] and 2) a display of forms which had been shattered and fragmented into a multi-spatial system of perspective. Many British artists, like their French contemporaries, no longer believed in the direct confrontation of nature; but Lewis and Bomberg went further and they approached a non-representational style. Although it is true that their elimination of a recognizable subject was still based on the Cubists' diagram, it is clear that the British painters departed radically from the Cubist position.

Futurism, both its theory and imagery, also figures in the emergence of this avant-garde.[3] A decisive rejection of the past is one of the principle tenets of the Vorticist manifesto, and a similar position was clearly stated by David Bomberg in the Foreword to his 1914 one-man show:

I look upon NATURE, while I live in a steel city . . . My
object is the *construction of Pure Form*. I reject everything in painting that is not Pure Form. I hate the colors
of the East, the Modern Medievalist and the Fat Man
of the Renaissance.[4]

The Vorticist painters and sculptors similarly embraced the iconography of Futurism, and "blessed,"
in the first issue of their magazine *Blast*, "machinery,
trains, steamships, all that distinguishes externally
our time."[5] Lewis and his ally Ezra Pound were not
willing to admit the influence that Futurist theory
and painting had on the development of Vorticism
and dogmatically claimed that they were "the inventors of this bareness and hardness." And while
Lewis attacked Marinetti—who had lectured in
London extensively between 1910 and 1914—Pound
valiantly denied any association with the Futurist
program.

Now you have Vorticism which is, roughly speaking,
Expressionism, neo-Cubism, and Imagism gathered into
one camp and Futurism in the other. . . . [Futurism] is
a spreading or surface art, as opposed to Vorticism
which is intensive.[6]

Pound's claim that Futurism was nothing more
than "accelerated impressionism," that it was a
"spreading art," leads one to believe that the poet
understood the Italians' concept of *ambiente*. Un-
fortunately he failed to observe that Wyndham

Lewis had borrowed extensively from the pictorial language of Boccioni in constructing his *Timon of Athens* portfolio. But in general, while the writings of Bomberg and Lewis show connections with the ideas of the Futurists, Vorticism and the new constructive geometric art were in fact closer in their formal language to Cubism.

The significance of avant-garde British painting during the first decades of the twentieth century stems not only from the fact that English artists were part of the "clustered burst of achievement"[7] that marked the flowering of easel painting at that time, but the specific achievement of Lewis and Bomberg is tied to the fact that they were the first to adopt a geometrically-oriented non-representational vocabulary. It is this contribution that needs clarification, for there emerged in British painting at that time two approaches to non-representation: the work of the Vorticists under the aegis of Wyndham Lewis and Ezra Pound, and the work of David Bomberg and Jacob Epstein labeled, by their apologist T. E. Hulme, as examples of a new constructive geometric art which was related to, yet distinct from, Vorticism. While it would be fruitful to point out the congruences of the literary and visual arts during this period it is not within the scope of this essay to discuss the effect that painters and sculptors had on poets. It should be remembered, however, that Pound and Hulme were instrumental in founding the Imagist school of poetry, and that certain theories—such as Pound's notion of "intensive manifolds"—developed from their interest in the visual arts. Furthermore, it should be noted that Hulme and Pound borrowed openly from each other's writings to justify their theories of visual art. While I have dealt elsewhere with the relationship of Pound's poetry to Vorticism,[8] I have not clarified T. E. Hulme's relationship to the work of David Bomberg and Jacob Epstein. It is this relationship which is the most interesting, principally because the art of David Bomberg emerges as the most sophisticated example of nonrepresentational painting in pre-war Britain.

T. E. Hulme was something of a self-taught poet-philosopher who had become interested in the visual arts. He had been instrumental in founding, with Ezra Pound, the Imagist school of poetry, publishing his "Complete Poetical Works" in the last section of Pound's *Ripostes* (1912). Four years earlier, Hulme had been the founder of the influential Poet's Club in London and by 1912 had become particularly interested in the sculpture of Jacob Epstein. Hulme had, in fact, purchased some of the sculptor's *Flenite Carvings*, finding in those abstract pieces a justification for his esthetic theories. By early 1914, Hulme had been commissioned to write a series of articles on modern art for *The New Age*, and in his first installment which appeared in January, the critic observed:

I am attempting to define the characteristics of a new constructive geometric art which seems to me to be

emerging at the present moment. . . . One might separate
the modern movement into three parts, to be roughly
indicated as Post-Impressionism, Analytical Cubism and
a new constructive geometric art . . . [the last] being
the only one containing possibilities of development.[9]

Hulme tended to equate Post-Impressionism with
the work of Roger Fry and his Omega Workshops,
Analytical Cubism with the work of the Vorticists
and the new constructive geometric art with the
work of Epstein and Bomberg. One week after this
first article appeared, Hulme gave a lecture to the
Quest Society in which he further elaborated the
characteristics of the new geometric art:

Expressed generally, there seems to be a desire for au-
sterity and bareness, a striving towards structure and
away from the messiness and confusion of nature and
natural things . . . I am thinking particularly of certain
pieces of sculpture I saw some years ago of Mr.
Epstein's.[10]

What is interesting about Hulme's position is that
it very clearly influenced Pound's ideas regarding
Vorticism. Reviewing the lecture by Hulme for
The Egoist, Pound observed: "My generation is not
the generation of the romanticists . . . To the present
condition of things we have nothing to say but
'*merde*,' and this new wild sculpture says it." [11]
Hulme's theories were undoubtedly not only an
important incentive for Epstein to experiment with

geometrical forms; they also reappeared in the manifestos of the Vorticists.

Hulme was more visually oriented than Pound, and was naturally drawn to esthetic theory, particularly as that discipline related to the visual arts. Pound developed his critical eye principally through his association with the Vorticists, particularly Wyndham Lewis and the sculptor Henri Gaudier-Brzeska. Yet while Pound later—in 1916—wrote the first critical study of Gaudier-Brzeska, the poet was willing to admit that "so far as I am concerned, Jacob Epstein was the first person who came talking about 'form.'" [12] Hulme, rather than Pound, had urged Epstein to experiment with geometrical shapes and to carve directly in brass, and his influence on the development of Epstein's abstract-geometrical work executed between 1912 and 1916 —culminating in *The Rock Drill*—was noted by R. H. Wilenski in 1928 when he observed:

After Hulme's death [in 1917], Epstein advanced upon the line of least resistance and developed his amazing power as a romantic modeler. [13]

It was only natural that Hulme would be drawn to the work of David Bomberg. By March, 1914, Bomberg was being cited by Hulme as representative of the "new tendencies" he first discovered in Epstein's *Flenite Carvings*. The one exhibiting society which brought together in one space the work of various factions of the British avant-garde was the newly formed London Group. In their March, 1914 exhibition, the work of Bomberg and Epstein as well as that of Lewis and the Vorticist painters and sculptors could be clearly assessed. It was at this show that the two most important works of Bomberg's geometrical phase were shown: *Ju-Jitsu* and *In the Hold*. The consensus of the critics who reviewed this major show of contemporary British art was that David Bomberg was surely the most articulate and advanced artist in London. Roger Fry noted that Bomberg was "evidently trying with immense energy and concentration to realize a new kind of plasticity. In his colossal patchwork design, there glimmers [in] a dazzling veil of black squares and triangles the suggestion of large volumes and movements . . . Mr. Bomberg is developing a quite distinct type of abstract design. . . . It would be rash to prophesy as yet, but . . . he has the . . . power to strike out a line on his own." [14] Even the conservative *Athenaeum* found Bomberg's *In the Hold* to be "the most entirely successful painting in the exhibition," having "the attraction which belongs to complete success." [15]

But it was T. E. Hulme who, in his third installment on Modern Art for the *New Age*, most clearly realized that Bomberg's paintings were the most satisfactory embodiments of his new constructive geometric art. Speaking of *In the Hold*, Hulme remarked that:

. . . the theory on which it is based seems to be this. In looking at a picture one never sees it as a whole, one's eye travels over it. In doing so, we continually find certain expectations fulfilled.[16]

And Hulme concluded: "I look forward . . . to Mr. Bomberg's future work with interest; he is undoubtedly an artist of remarkable quality." [17] It is little wonder that Wyndham Lewis was anxious to bring David Bomberg more fully into the Vorticist movement. And it is also clear that Bomberg was simply not interested.

What is of interest is that while Hulme favored the work of Epstein and Bomberg, he admitted that the Vorticists had also contributed to the new geometrical art. Yet at the same time he was praising Bomberg and admitting the contributions of the Vorticists to the development of the new constructive geometric art, Hulme was critical of the work of Wyndham Lewis. For Hulme, Lewis' works did not "produce as a whole, the kind of coherent effect which, according to theory, they ought to produce. The forms are not controlled enough." [18] Accordingly, one must see Bomberg's work of 1913 and 1914, together with the theories of T. E. Hulme, as influential models upon which the non-representational phase of Vorticism was based. In fact, it is not too far-fetched to claim that Ezra Pound's "Vorticist" poem which appeared in *Blast* as "DOG-MATIC STATEMENT ON THE GAME AND PLAY OF CHESS

Constructive Geometric Art in London, 1910–15
(THEME FOR A SERIES OF PICTURES)" is a verbal ana-
logue based on Bomberg's *Ju-Jitsu:*

Red knights, brown bishops, bright queens
Striking the board, falling in strong "L's" of color,
Reaching and striking in angles,
    Holding lines of one color:
This board is alive with light
Those pieces are living in form,
      Their moves break and reform the pattern: . . .[19]

Herbert Read, in one of his first poems, seems to
have been similarly influenced by one of the wood-
cuts of the Vorticist artist, Edward Wadsworth,
when he wrote:

    Above the vibrant town,
    Above its dull clamor,
    Roofs like ragged blades
    Break into the moist golden glow,
    With mosaic of lustreful tiles
    And slates that gleam metallic.
    Outward from me
    Electric wires traverse and ray
    I sit like a spider in its web
    And tranquilly survey
    The slanting planes that round me swirl
    In iridescent aureole.[20]

Hulme's contributions were essentially those of a
theoretician. He articulated—as Apollinaire and
Marinetti had done for Cubism and Futurism—an

esthetic position which upon closer inspection was almost entirely derivative. Hulme never hid the fact that he admired the popular *Abstraction and Empathy* of the German esthetician Wilhelm Worringer, and he had several times traveled to Germany to meet the distinguished scholar. Worringer's rather simplistic, polar theory of art reduced all visual manifestations to organic or geometrical cultural positions. Thus, when Worringer observed that certain sculpture of the "geometrical" view showed a "maximum compactness of material, forcible compression of the object into geometrical or cubic regularity," [21] Hulme paraphrased the idea in explaining the work of Jacob Epstein. Although Hulme adopted Worringer's position, he also introduced his "theory of unity" which he first used when criticizing the work of Wyndham Lewis:

His [Lewis'] sense of form seems to be segment rather than integral, by which I mean that one form probably springs out of the preceding one as he works, instead of being conceived as part of a whole.[22]

Comparing the work of Bomberg and Lewis seems to be a question of contrasting temperaments. Both employed primary colors, both tended to use surface patterns based on angular and geometrical configurations. Yet where Lewis becomes reductive, Bomberg becomes additive in the handling of planes and of perspective and in the use of figure-ground relationships. The distinction between the work of Bomberg and Lewis—and this holds true for the differences between the new constructive geometric art and Vorticism—is a distinction based on control, complexity, facility and unity. Bomberg, of all the avant-garde artists working at the time, made his paintings work most convincingly.

Seen in the context of Continental developments prior to World War I, the work of the British artists might appear a bit mean, but in the context of British painting, Lewis and Bomberg severely and irrevocably broke with the academic position in England and with the supremacy that Post-Impressionism had at the time.

In a larger framework, Bomberg and Lewis provided a basis for the emerging British Constructivism of the early '30s. For the inventors of this "bareness and hardness" pointed out that they were indeed the great "enemies of Romance." As such, Bomberg and Lewis expelled, in the words of Ezra Pound, "extraneous matter out of . . . art." [23] The result for British art was a refinement and purification.

1. John Berger, "The Moment of Cubism," *New Left Review*, 42 (March/April, 1967), p. 76.

2. *Ibid.*, p. 85. "The metaphorical model of Cubism is the *diagram*: the diagram being a visible, symbolic representation of invisible processes, forces, structures."

3. For a detailed account of the relationship between Futurism and Vorticism, see William C. Lipke, "Futurism and the Development of Vorticism," *Studio International*, V. 173, N. 188 (April, 1967), pp. 173-179.

4. David Bomberg, "Foreword, Works by David Bomberg." Chenil Gallery, London (July, 1914). The complete text is reprinted in William C. Lipke, *David Bomberg* (London, 1967), p. 118. It should be noted that Bomberg and Epstein were the only two members of the British avant-garde to have one-man shows prior to 1915.

5. "Initial Manifesto," *Blast* VI, (July, 1914), pp. 40-41.

6. Ezra Pound, "Vorticism," *Fortnightly Review*, 96, DLXXIII (Sept. 1, 1914), p. 464.

7. The phrase is that of George Kubler. See his *The Shape of Time* (New Haven, 1962), Chapter One.

8. See William C. Lipke and Bernard W. Rozran, "Ezra Pound and Vorticism: A Polite Blast," *Wisconsin Studies in Contemporary Literature*, VII, 2 (Summer, 1966), pp. 201-210.

9. T. E. Hulme, "Modern Art I. The Grafton Group," *The New Age*, XIV, ii (January 15, 1914), pp. 341-342.

10. T. E. Hulme, "Modern Art and Its Philosophy," reprinted in *Speculations* (ed. Herbert Read), New York (n.d.), pp. 96, 82.

11. Ezra Pound, "The New Sculpture," *The Egoist*, 1, 4 (February 16, 1914), pp. 67-68.

12. Ezra Pound, "Affirmations III: Jacob Epstein," *The Egoist*, XVI, 12 (January 21, 1915), pp. 311-312.

13. R. H. Wilenski, *The Meaning of Modern Sculpture* (New York, 1961). Originally published in 1928. Pp. 103-104.

14. Roger Fry, "Two Views of the London Group," *The Nation* (March 14, 1914), pp. 998-999.

15. "The London Group," *The Athenaeum*, N. 4507 (March 14, 1914), p. 387.

16. T. E. Hulme, "Modern Art III: The London Group," *The New Age* (March 26, 1914), p. 662.

17. *Ibid.*, p. 662.

18. *Ibid.*, p. 661.

19. Ezra Pound, "Dogmatic Statement . . ." *Blast, II* (July, 1915), p. 19.

20. Herbert Read, "Roofs," *Arts and Letters*, I, 3, (January, 1918), p. 109.

21. Wilhelm Worringer, *Abstraction and Empathy* (trans. by Michael Bullock), (New York, 1953), p. 89. The book had already gone into its third printing by 1910.

22. T. E. Hulme, "Modern Art III: The London Group," p. 661.

23. Ezra Pound, "Vorticism," p. 464.

Collective, Ideological, Combative

by Harold Rosenberg

Well-known critic Harold Rosenberg, prolific writer
on various aspects of various avant-gardes, is currently
art critic for *The New Yorker*, and is on the graduate
faculty of the University of Chicago. His books
include *The Tradition of the New*, *The Anxious Object*,
Arshile Gorky, *Artworks and Packages*.

"Where are the avant-gardes?"
FIDEL CASTRO. HAVANA, 1968.

DEALERS, critics, collectors, museum directors also keep asking the question of Fidel Castro. But they are more easily satisfied. Every few years they find an avant-garde. Each time, however, there is something vaguely unsatisfactory about it, something unreal and fabricated—an avant-garde made to order, to meet the demand. As for a true vanguard ... there is, first of all, the question, What is it?

The key is the ideological community, that is to say, a collective movement based on certain intellectual presuppositions. An individual can be an innovator, but there is no such thing as an avant-garde individual, except as follower or leader. Melville was not avant-garde though his thinking in *Bartleby* and parts of *Pierre* was a century ahead of his time. Nor was Poe; he became avant-garde posthumously when the Symbolists invested him with a halo. Those who are looking for avant-gardes are looking for a convinced *crowd*. An individual who is an innovator spies upon the unknown, but only a phalanx can take up a forward position. Cézanne is not avant-garde, Cubism is.

It can be asserted, then, that art does not need avant-gardes (it can get along through individuals), but society does need them if ideas are to prevail. The avant-garde represents a common direction for the future—for example, the domination by science of all human conditions, including love, dreaming and the response to color. Vanguard art tends to sketch the outlines of a dogma, or a set of convictions.

Actions, both individual and collective, often occur spontaneously, that is, through the promptings of tradition and temperament. But spontaneous actions carry no insignia of advanced status. No one knows where they belong in relation to time and progress. No matter how radical its effects, an action is not avant-garde without an ideology to characterize it. The Paris Commune became an exemplary avant-garde political event when Karl Marx hailed it as a working model of the future society.

More unequivocally avant-garde than actions retrospectively labeled advanced is the action that *arises out of* the ideology. With most twentieth-century avant-gardes the ideology comes first and shapes the action, as well as accrediting it. Despite Marx, the Leninist "vanguard of the proletariat" denied that any spontaneous action could result in social advance without the intervention of the Party. Are rioting students avant-garde? Only those who carry a Party card or Chairman Mao's little red book.

Today's art-historical painting-sculpture vanguard is of the same conviction; with it, ideology, the blueprint of end and means, precedes creation, is the basis of creation. More, in the Constructivist-derived avant-gardism, creation is often nothing more than the working out in paint or metal of an ideological conclusion.

The first quality of avant-garde art is newness. Newness itself can produce scandal, polemic, mystification—in sum, supply the major qualities of vanguard art. But newness wears off, and with it the scandal and the mystery. The avant-garde work becomes quality-less. Logically, it should then be destroyed, or destroy itself. The idea of the short life of a work of art belongs to the epoch of the avant-gardes. But instead of being destroyed the work is salvaged by art history. This violates its avant-garde essence and compels it to deny itself.

Recently a new avant-garde argument has been adduced, one that comes directly out of art-historical thinking. Since the avant-garde work is destined to become quality-less, why not *begin* with an art of no qualities? The avant-garde headed by such artists as Stella and Judd is praised for having achieved the elimination of feeling, illusion, etc., for having produced works belonging to the same order as things habitually overlooked. This is another way of praising these art-history-conscious artists for being interested in nothing but the shortest route to the front.

Avant-garde art is art not seen before; if it retains that characteristic after it has become familiar, it is not only avant-garde art but good art. To hold a lasting position in the art of an epoch, works need another kind of newness than that of being advanced. In *Finnegan's Wake* the novelty of form matches the dissolution of human identity into the ocean of language-gestures. In this larger conception of a work related to its time, what counts is the idea and the modification of the medium to embody that idea. Generation after generation can go forward to a Cézanne or a Dostoyevsky.

But the embodied idea is always the product of an individual; the collective, the movement, can grasp the idea only as an abstraction and through imitating the model of an abstraction. In the ideological community the new is not the unique (which can manifest itself in the familiar); the new is the historically necessary, the next step as determined by the ideology. Such newness in painting is, for example, the elimination of illusory depth, though the flatness thus achieved is characteristic of pattern ornamentation, and is not new at all outside of art.

Evidently, the new as creation and the new as avant-garde are not always the same thing. The mind of the creator enters into communion with minds of all times and places; the avant-garde mind is fixed on thoughts leading to the ideologically determined next step.

The creator acts on the assumption that in drawing on all available energies, he is bound to be in tune with the time, that his move is the correct move for the moment in which he acts. His insight into time is embedded in his practice. In contrast, the avant-gardist has an *idea* of the present as a means of transition to the future; instead of communing with the present as the container of the past and the possible, he seeks to use it to fulfill the commands of his system. The rhythm of the avant-garde is the forward drive from a Now defined in terms of science, technology, history. It thins out time to a line leading to a predictable result. It wishes to surpass the moment and shake off or demolish its inherited content.

The creator recovers the moment which avant-gardes have passed over, bringing to light the demons lurking in it to frustrate the forward march of the idea. (The great moderns, from Baudelaire to Kafka or Beckett, are enveloped in uneasiness, but art movements, with the possible exception of Expressionism, are optimistic.) No important art is ever only of Now, as no Now is only of Now.

Embedded, as we have said, in practice, the creator's insight into time cannot be transferred to the ideological community as a whole—it was, for example, futile for Trotsky to demonstrate that "the rhythm of events" in France and Spain in the '30s called for certain actions. Nor could Pollock have explained why the time had come for switching to his drip technique. The avant-garde, however, sees Trotsky or Pollock as engaged in ideological calculations which those armed with advanced conceptions can evaluate, and either reject or carry to the next phase. The image of a Pollock consciously planning to bring about an advance in pictorial space is an absurdity typical of avant-garde conceptions of change.

In subsuming individuals under movements, avant-garde styles aim at two antithetical qualities. On the one hand, they seek to recover the freshness and surprise of the innovations that gave rise to the movements; on the other, to affirm the rationale of the movement as representing a new order. These impulses cannot be reconciled. The phenomenon of surprise accompanies images plucked out of the unknown; that of the new order, images projected by a logic based on certainties. The first implies a continual search, the second the affirmation of known necessities.

As a result of the basic opposition between its conceptions of the new and of the advanced, each avant-garde movement consists of two camps and is always on the verge of going to war with itself, if not actually at war. It is the inner conflict between creation and system that puts an end to the movements. Thus besides being collective and ideological, avant-gardes are by nature combative. Each is bent on destroying its predecessor and stands on guard against being replaced by newcomers. The avant-gardes have brought into art the dynamics of radical politics. Their intellectual do-or-die is a major contribution; it makes art a serious pursuit and keeps it from degenerating into mere craft. It is by the context of its conflicts that the level of a political or esthetic movement is identified—for example, the battle of the American art vanguards of the past decade against Abstract-Expressionism, but not against American society or the growing art bureaucracy, prevents taking them seriously.

Historically, the primary antagonist of the avant-garde is the middle class. From the start, avant-garde art movements have paralleled advanced political movements. The term "avant-garde" was coined by social philosophers after the construction of a new order had been thrown open to competition by the French Revolution. An elite of artists, Saint-Simon thought, would march in the van of representatives of all the intellectual faculties capable of contributing to the social good.

The attitude of the artists themselves toward this role of changing the world has been an ambiguous one. All avant-gardes like to claim that their art *does* something, if only isolate itself from the ennui, sentimentalism or illusoriness of daily life. But while some art movements have conducted direct attacks on the conditions of life (e.g. Realism, Surrealism), others (Neo-Impressionism, Symbolism) have been content to believe that life could be changed by changing art.

In both instances, opposition to the existing order is implicit. The politics of an avant-garde art movement might consist of nothing more rebellious than overthrowing the conviction of the middle class that color in a painting ought to correspond to that of appearances. Yet by violating its esthetic, and at times moral, beliefs, avant-gardist art movements have played upon the nervous system of the middle class with intimations of a coming new order in everything.

Hence for a century sympathy (often without understanding) could be taken for granted between esthetic and political vanguards, though it is usually difficult to trace the influence of radical political ideas in the art works, or the influence of radical esthetic insights in the politics. This tacit assumption of parallel hopes for a renovated world reached expression in the Bolshevik Revolution, hailed by avant-gardists of several art movements. With the suppression of avant-gardist art by the Communists in the '20s, the political and esthetic vanguards split apart for the first time.

Bolshevism, and later Nazism, offered avant-garde art the alternative of supporting a revolutionary regime through esthetic conformity (that is, through ceasing to exist) or attempting to revolutionize itself without any prospect of changing life, in view of the superior force of the "professional revolutionists."

Either of these choices could only lead to the end of avant-gardism. Without its political shadow, the defiance of accepted social or moral norms becomes a game in which the old threats are turned into an insider's joke. Today, revolts restricted to the esthetic are welcomed by the middle class as a solace; they revive the aroma of the exciting times when hostility and misunderstanding between artists and the public were considered dangerous.

With the door to politics closed by totalitarianism art has to an increasing degree affirmed its dissociation from political and social purpose. In the ideologies of recent art movements art-historical reasoning has been offered as a substitute for consciousness of history. In this parody of vanguardism, which revives the academic idea of art as a separate "realm," art can make revolutionary strides without causing a ripple on the streets or in the mind of a collector.

Not content with renouncing radical aims, the new academic vanguard casts suspicion on the social and intellectual radicalism of past vanguards. In the current rewriting of art history the interest of advanced artists of the past in nature, science, action was a pretense disguising the will to contribute to problems of form.

The final confirmation of the split between political and esthetic radicalism came at the 1968 Venice Biennale when militant students denounced the advanced art presented there as "art for dealers and the rich," and carried signs advising onlookers to "visit the pavilion of the police." Cut off from the will to change the world, art today, whatever its merit, is not avant-garde, and claims of affiliation with the vanguardism of the past are a sham exploiting the radical tradition. For the present, avant-gardes and ideologies are dead, and the only force for the new in art is the individual in his erratic communion with other individuals.

Futurism: The Avant-Garde as a Way of Life

by Joshua Taylor

Joshua Taylor, Director of the National Collection of
Fine Arts, Smithsonian Institution, Washington, D.C.,
organized the major show of Futurism at the
Museum of Modern Art, New York, and wrote the
definitive catalogue for that influential event.

*"But we will hear no more about the past,
we young, strong Futurists!"*

Looked at in the cold light of 50 years after, the manifesto that launched the doctrine of Futurism, published on the front page of *Le Figaro* in Paris in February, 1909, remains a provocative but puzzling document. Couched more in the language of politics than of art, it none the less expressed a euphoric mood and set a goal that was ultimately esthetic. But it is hard to disentangle the language from the goal, the politics from the art; and Marinetti, whose brainchild the entire movement was, although he always spoke of "we," made no effort to distinguish them. On the contrary, following a principle well established in the nineteenth century, he believed that the one found basis in the other: that social change was necessary for art and that art, in turn, could provoke social change.

Yet remarkably enough, no art seems less imbued with social content than that of the painters who came together under the Futurist banner early in 1910: Boccioni, Carrà, Russolo, Severini, Balla and the early associates, Romani and Bonzagni. Nor was its form seen at once as revolutionary. In fact, those critics who were already kindled by the succession of startling visual transformations that had changed the course of art over the preceding 20 years found the first Futurist painting disappointingly tame in comparison with the verbal promise. While it was often appealing and sometimes moving, it provided little shock either in its subject matter or its form. Unlike the vicious pronouncements—for burning museums and praising war—Futurist art was persuasive rather than combative; rather than destruction it offered positive, vigorous pleasure.

But the discrepancy between what Marinetti said and what the Futurist painters did was not the result of limited capacity nor of faulty conviction. While Marinetti formulated his ideas in social terms, judging his success by the violence of public reaction (sometimes real, sometimes imagined), the painters were concerned with color and shape and their personal response to the perceptual world. The exhilaration of the avant-garde pervaded both—and

Boccioni, for one, was happy to join Marinetti in flag-burnings and other riot-provoking acts—but the social and the artistic avant-garde rarely share more than the excitement derived from a sense of advancing against a foe. Yet the belief that they were pushing forward, ahead of their own society, breaking social bonds of restraint, seemed of particular importance to the artists in reaffirming their individual esthetic sensibilities. To negate an imaginary public was important in taking the positive step toward a new personal awareness. As in most such instances, the public, in so far as it impinged on art, was largely a myth created by the artists themselves. Although the Futurists carried their activities more to the actual public than did most succeeding movements, staging dramatic assaults on the public complacency in theaters, opera houses and public squares, they had no more appreciable effect on public action or taste than the Brücke in Germany or the Vorticists in England.

To be sure, a public such as they described doubtless existed—" . . . you do not even remember having lived!" the Futurists told them with scorn—but this was not the public that would respond to their dicta and art. Surely their aim was not to reform so useful an opponent; their exhilaration depended on the lethargy of the mass on which they heaped their ridicule. The concept of avant-garde is postulated on the image of the retardataire. For the Italian group, the image was defined in the dimension of time: they were avant-garde because allied with the future in a world of change; their enemy was the past. Therefore the public, the government, society at large were *passatisti*.

If it has any lasting effect at all as spokesman or theorist for art, social avant-gardism serves only to stimulate artistic creation, and the works produced ultimately stand or fall on a basis other than social or political. While one might trace a nascent Fascism in some of the writings of Marinetti, there are no such intimations in the highly personal art of Boccioni. After all, social and artistic revolutions are different in kind: in art, to be in the forefront of change means to alter one's capacity—"we are . . . the primitives of a new and completely transformed sensibility," the Futurist painters declared in 1910; in society, it means to change one's opportunities, the environment.

But what was the nature of this new sensibility, built upon the image of a new society? In the first place, it was a sensibility based on the awareness of continuous change, a change of which the individual himself was at every moment a part. The projected new society, with its speeding autos and puffing engines, was less the source than the symbol of the phenomenon. It is not to be wondered at that the subject matter of the Futurist painters so little reflected the society they extolled; their art was meant to speed as fast as motor cars, not represent motor cars speeding. Although Balla painted dashing automobiles, he painted at least as many studies of flying swifts, and Boccioni chose the horse and the athlete as his pictorial images since they more readily translated the idea of speed into personal bodily motion. None of the Italian painters conceived of man as a machine, regardless of how much pleasure machines gave them in heightening the sense of their own "physical transcendence." The machine provided an extension of man's physical capabilities; but, possibly more important, it broke down traditional concepts of the physical limits of human action and, eventually, of the mind. With the machine as a symbol, the imagination was suddenly free to push in any direction with the assurance that the technical frontier was not far behind. A gesture was not as long as an arm but as extensive as immeasurable time. Thinking, communication, worked with the magic speed of telegraphy; the "wireless imagination" was Marinetti's term.

The first preoccupation of the artists was to develop their paintings as evocative symbols, fields of action in which the artist/spectator, rather than a representative agent, becomes the chief player. Through 1910 and 1911 they tried various means to get into their own paintings, to identify themselves with their plastic environment. "We will put the spectator into the middle of the painting," they had declared confidently. But the problem became increasingly complex as they recognized new levels of identification. Boccioni's and Carrà's contact late in

1911 with Cubist painting was useful in breaking their dependence on gestural lines and posed new possibilities of structure, advantages of which Severini had long since been aware. But they were impatient with the fact that the Cubist painters, especially those around Gleizes and Metzinger, engaged the attention of the viewer with their broken forms only to weave from the resulting erratic motion a pleasantly static and limited fabric. Rather than capitalize on the sense of change derived from their analysis of perception, complained Boccioni and Carrà, the French painters were content to show how it could be organized into new forms which were no less static nor hermetic than the forms of objects with which they had begun. In their angry criticism of 1912 and 1913, the Italians insisted that the artist should provoke a sense of dynamic change in order to live within it, not to organize it back into harmony and equilibrium. Reason must not dominate the unreasonableness of change.

While Gleizes saw his painting as moving toward a greater realization of universal harmony, toward an epic oneness, Boccioni saw his work simply as moving. To embody the fact of change was his triumph, not to spur change toward a goal. Regardless of the political application of Futurist ideas, esthetically they stood for continuous revolution as a way of art. Art was an act of unceasing expansion and freedom, not of order and limit.

Once the painters had grasped the possibilities

of formal persuasiveness—and Boccioni lamented that in his isolation he had had to re-create the history of modern art for himself—they moved rapidly to reconsider the implications of their initial pronouncements. Simple physical involvement early gave way in Boccioni to "states of mind," which in turn took on the complexity of simultaneous seeing and remembering, sights and sounds, words and pictorial form. Any means of apprehension was judged valid. But fresh apprehension required surprise. The destruction of every expected syntax, of form or subject matter, became a positive principle of operation. The new syntax was no syntax: a situation had to be created in which meanings and relationships would constantly change. Severini's theory of plastic analogies of 1913 provides an example. The rhythms of a dancer might become the rhythms of the sea, only to become those of a bouquet of flowers, and so on. Although Boccioni's striding sculptures of 1912–13 clearly recall human figures, each form was determined as a synthetic presentation of solid mass interacting with space, further complicated by light and movement until all stability of substance was lost. And Boccioni insisted that the individual elements could not be isolated by analysis; using Bergsonian terminology he pointed out that the synthesis took place within the intuition, sensitive to change, and to single out one element or order, whether of vision or memory, would be to violate the expanding and freely creative activity of the mind. The motion of the object only partly interested him; it was uninhibited freedom of the mind—possibly while contemplating a head in front of a window or a bottle on a table—that proved him and the willing spectator to be part of the active, hence modern, world.

Thinking, seeing, remembering were all part of any single moment of experience, and soon to the usual means were added sound (Russolo and Pratella began their experiments with noise machines and multi-rhythmic music in 1912), smell (which seems not to have extended beyond the manifesto stage) and onomatopoeic and evocative words. Marinetti published his technical manifesto of Futurist literature in 1912 and further clarified it in May, 1913, discarding grammatical order, verbal connectives and specific verb forms—"free word" literature, he called it. Severini and Carrà quickly followed with "free word" painting. The distinction between painting and poetry became merely academic.

As a kind of climax to the euphoric progress of Futurist thought, Balla and a young proselyte, Fortunato Depero, published in March, 1915, two months before Italy entered the World War, a summarizing document modestly titled, "The Futurist Reconstruction of the Universe." Basic to the declaration was the notion that painting, even as expanded with words, was no longer adequate. Art,

they said, must exist in all three dimensions and
be:

1. Abstract 2. Dynamic (relative [cinematic] plus absolute motion) 3. Very Transparent (through the velocity
and volatility of the plastic complex which must appear
and disappear lightly and impalpably) 4. Filled with
Color and Luminous (using an interior light) 5. Auton-
omous (that is, bearing likeness only to itself) 6. Trans-
formable 7. Dramatic 8. Volatile 9. Odorous 10. Noisy
(plastic noise simultaneous with plastic expression) 11.
Explosive (simultaneous explosive appearance and disappearance).

Art was to draw upon all of the new techniques and
materials of science and commerce: it must be an
art of discovery in a new world. Light, motors, trans-
parencies, all contributed to provoke surprise,
wonder and delight. And of necessity, art was no
longer than, but just as transient as, life itself.

These ideas, not dissimilar from those of Sant'Elia
concerning the new architecture, published in 1914,
come from Balla, the oldest of the Futurists, but
they point to the new generation. Boccioni, in spite
of his startling sculpture manifesto and continuing
political activity, depended more and more on his
painterly sensibility, and Carrà, after his final series
of collages published as *Guerrapittura* in 1915, with-
drew into a contemplative world that found expression only after his encounter with de Chirico. The
political manifesto that Marinetti, Boccioni, Carrà

and Russolo had signed in 1913 is far from the direction their art had taken and sounds chillingly like later proclamations of the Fascist state.

The artists, working to destroy the past, convention, all inhibitions, wrapped them together in a mythical image of an inert society, not in order to found a new and more efficacious social order, but to be able to engage in the excitement of continuous creativity. Art, for the Futurists, was to be not a thing but a process of becoming, constantly pushing beyond the limits, always ahead. "Erect upon the summit of the world," they shouted, "we hurl our challenge to the stars."

But the war changed the world. Many of the young men who began to exhibit under the Futurist banner in Rome in 1914 had not come through the end-of-century crisis of identity but took the new technological world as a natural environment. The airplane, not the horse or the motorcar, became their symbol, and with it came a new sense of abstraction and organizational power. Boccioni and Sant'Elia, both killed in 1916, were evoked as saints and precursors of the new movements, both artistic and political. Politics and art are much alike, said Mussolini at the opening of an exhibition in 1926, because they are both creative. Marinetti, an active supporter of the new regime and member of the new Academy of Italy, continued to sponsor art as social assault, especially through the theater. But ironically, the searching self-realization of the "First

Futurism" was kept alive not in the noisy mechanism of *aeropittura* or other self-consciously progressive efforts, but in the silence of the *Scuola Meta-
fisica*, the whispered still-lifes of Morandi and the
brooding archaeology of Mario Sironi.

Notes on a
Lost Avant-Garde:
Architecture,
U.S.S.R., 1920-30

by Kenneth Frampton

Kenneth Frampton was a practicing architect and
technical editor of the review *Architectural Design* in
London before coming to this country in 1965,
where he has successively occupied the post of
visiting lecturer and, since 1966, of associate professor
at the School of Architecture, Princeton University.

Few projects in the history of contemporary architecture can compare in their impact or their latent influence to Vladimir Tatlin's 1920 design for a monument to the Third Internationale. In Russian avant-garde culture of this century, it occupies a position as a work of "architecture" comparable to that held in painting by Malevich's 1912 designs for Kruchenik's Futurist play *Victory over the Sun*, out of which Suprematism immediately emerged. The importance of Tatlin's tower has now been generally acknowledged by architectural historians, yet even today, few are willing to recognize the extent to which it crystallized a new consciousness which was to function as a continuous line of

thought, sometimes covert, sometimes overt, in the
development of European architecture between the
two world wars. Central to this partially sub-
terranean tradition was Tatlin's now well-known
"Program of the Productivist Group," also published
in 1920, partly in response to the much more famous
"Realist Manifesto" issued a few months previous
by the brothers Gabo and Pevsner. The significance
of this program lay in its conscious coinage of the
term "Constructivism," which it had the temerity to
define. The term, since then much misused, was
given a rather exact formulation by those who invented it. The Productivist Group based the definition of Constructivism upon the subsequent
definition of two additional compound terms, *"tektonika"* and *"faktura"*; the first referring to a
complex of societal and industrial techniques, the
second to the synthetic "objectivity" of its unim-
peded realization.

"Tektonika" is derived from the structure of communism
and the effective exploitation of industrial matter. Construction is organization. It accepts the contents of the
matter itself, already formulated. Construction is formulating activity taken to the extreme, allowing, however,
for further "tektonical" work. The matter deliberately
chosen and effectively used, without however hindering
the progress of construction or limiting the "tektonika,"
is called *"faktura"* by the group.[1]

From this it is possible to deduce that Constructivism was first and foremost seen as the act of

construction conceived primarily as the organization of a total technical capacity, specifically to be compounded out of Communism and industrialization. This manifestation of constructed or organized technique was thought of as the *fact*, or the *objective* inevitable actuality of Constructivism. The Constructivists regarded their raw material first of all as physical matter in general, consciously acknowledging its inherent nature and mode of production, and secondly as intellectual matter, that is, as light, plane, space, color and volume. According to one contemporary critic, Alexei Gan, the Constructivists were to treat intellectual and solid materials in the same way. Somewhat in the manner of today's Red Guards, the Productionists (i.e. the Constructivists) were categorically against any gradual transition from ancient forms to the new scientific socialist mode of building. Their mood was apocalyptical. They were polemically extreme in their opposition to both art and religion. Their slogans extolled with almost Futurist fervor the virtues of industrial technology and socialist collectivity. They stood for an unmitigated utilitarianism, as may be seen from a later and more succinct definition of Constructivism that appeared in the Constructivist magazine LEF in 1923. This definition reads as follows:

Constructivism is the organization of the given material on the principles of tektonics, structure and construction, the form becoming defined in the process of creation, by the utilitarian aim of the object.[2]

Tatlin's Monument to the Third Internationale characterizes this intention to consider *intellectual* and *physical* raw materials as equal elements in any given assembly or construction. However, one can hardly consider *its* form as having been creatively "defined through the utilitarian aim of the object." In spite of the anti-art, anti-religion sloganeering of the Productivists, one can only consider the Tatlin Tower as primarily a symbolic structure. According to architect Berthold Lubetkin, a model of the tower was first exhibited under a ribbon which bore the slogan, "Engineers Create New Forms"; this ribbon was later borne through the streets by crowds of enthusiastic students. The millennialistic mechanico-idolatry of this project is clearly manifest in a contemporary description of it, which presumably paraphrases Tatlin's own words:

The whole monument rests on two main axes which are closely connected. In the direction of these axes an upward movement is accomplished; this is crossed transversely at each of its points by the movement of the spirals. . . . The chambers are arranged vertically above one another and surrounded by various harmonious structures. [Here the writer is referring to the glazed mobile elements contained within the superstructure.] By means of special machinery they are to be kept in perpetual motion but at different speeds. The lower chamber is *cubiform* and turns on its axis once a year; it is to be used for legislative purposes. . . . The chamber above this is *pyramidal* in shape and makes one revolution a month; this is for the meetings of assemblies and executive bodies. Finally the third and highest part of the building is in the shape of a *cylinder* and turns on its axis once a day. This part of the building will be used chiefly for administration and propaganda, that is, as a bureau of information, for newspapers, manifestos, etc. Telegraphs, radio-apparatus and projectors for cinematographic performances will be installed in this chamber. . . .

In itself the use of spirals for monumental architecture means an enrichment of composition. Just as the triangle, as an image of general equilibrium, is the best expression of the Renaissance, so the spiral is the most effective symbol of the modern spirit of the age . . . while the dynamic line of bourgeois society, aiming at possession of the land and the soil, was the horizontal, the spiral, which, rising from the earth, detaches itself from all animal, earthly and oppressing interests, forms the purest expression of humanity set free by the revolution. . . . The monument unites the legislative with the executive and with the act of information; to each of these functions a position in space has been assigned corresponding to its nature. In this way and also by means of the chief building material used, the purity and clearness of initiative and its freedom from all material encumbrance is symbolically indicated. . . .

Just as the product of the number of oscillations and the wavelength is the spatial measure of sound, so the proportion between glass and iron is the measure of material rhythm. By the union of these two fundamentally important materials, a compact and imposing simplicity and, at the same time, relation, is expressed, since these materials, for both of which fire is the creator of life, form the elements of modern art. By their union, rhythms must be created of mighty power, as though an ocean were being born. By the transformation of these forms into reality, dynamics will be embodied in unsurpassable magnificence, just as the pyramids once and for all expressed the principle of statics.[3]

This passage with its Promethean evaluation of iron and glass is rather typical of that peculiar mixture of millennialistic symbolism and utilitarian dialectic which abounds in the rhetoric of the Russian avant-garde during the immediate post-Revolutionary period. Sentences such as "rhythms must be created of mighty power, as though an ocean were being born" are obviously indebted to the Futurist Marinetti, while the writer's reference to the pyramids is reminiscent of Eiffel's appeal to the precedent of Egyptian monumentality, in publicly defending the design of his famous tower in 1885. Tatlin no doubt saw his own monumental project not only as an homage to Eiffel, but also as an almost cabalistic celebration of the Revolution with its use of the three Platonic solids, the latent magic number principle, the logarithmic spiral, etc. This spiral form, symbolizing the transcendental dynamism of the Revolution, was to occur again and again, as a constant motive in Soviet avant-garde work throughout the next decade.

The symbolic use of an ascending spiral has obvious antique and archaic precedents in the commemorative column and the apotropaic labyrinth, but its use in the modern era (i.e., post-1750) seems always to have been indicative of a transcendental symbolism of secular "socialist" content. A demonstration of this is to be found in Carola Giedion-Welcker's study of contemporary sculpture wherein Tatlin's Tower is convincingly juxtaposed with Hermann Obrist's monument of 1902 and Rodin's project for a monument to labor of 1897. To this remarkable series one might venture to add Etienne Boullée's late 18th-century design for a truncated cone-shaped tower, which like the Obrist monument features a procession of figures with linked hands spiraling up toward its summit.

Tatlin's Tower was the initial symbolic crystallization of a Constructivist esthetic which on subsequent occasions would occur as the direct expression of a utilitarian rationale. The use of industrial materials, the expression of literal movement, the emphasis on dynamic form, the direct exposure of both structure and function, the fusion of "paleo" with "neo" technology, combined with the direct incorporation of daily information and propaganda, reflected the ethos of a secular era dedicated to the rationalization of human life through organized industrialization.

Typical of the direct development of this esthetic in the service of an actual building program was the Vesnin brothers' 1923 project for the Pravda Newspaper Building, of which the Russian avant-garde graphist and architect El Lissitzky wrote in 1929 as follows:

All the accessories of the city street such as signs, advertisements, loudspeakers, etc. are integrated into this building. They are treated as equal elements in the design and assembled into an entity. This is the esthetic of Constructivism.[4]

In this small building, about 19 by 19 feet in plan, the Vesnin brothers projected a clear expression of a skeleton frame, behind whose glazed skin twin elevators would have shuttled back and forth to serve each of its six floors. The whole building was clearly meant to be understood as an industrial product in which the mobile elements such as doors, windows, elevators, etc. were of the same component caliber as the ancillary equipment—the red flag, the searchlight, the numerical clock, the loudspeaker and the rotating billboard.

This project seen in retrospect holds its own as a "canonical" work with other avant-garde European projects of comparable date, such as Le Corbusier's Ozenfant studio, Rietveld's Schroeder house or Mies van der Rohe's glass skyscraper project, all of the years 1922–23. The essentially "synthetic" nature of Constructivism is made explicit by this comparison; the Pravda project is the only work consciously designed to assimilate into its form an extensive range of non-architectural media.

The direct structural articulation of the Pravda Building, the transparency of its façade, the expressive mobility of its components and the empirical determination of its arrangement are each in turn characteristic of the Constructivist esthetic as it was to evolve during the early '20s. The underlying utilitarian rationale led frequently to mechanistic fantasia which often made such an idealization of the appearance of utility as to involve a sacrifice in actual convenience. The aristocracy of the avantgarde could well afford in the early years of Soviet *Sturm und Drang* to be indifferent to such issues as commodity or economy. Far more important for many designers, in the heat of the unrealizable moment, was an imaginative vigor equal to the iconoclastic appeal of everyday polemics. In such a climate the initial principles of the Productivist program were often misinterpreted or deliberately abandoned. Only artists of high caliber and conviction such as Tatlin and Rodchenko were able throughout the 'twenties, by working as "industrial designers," to produce a range of utilitarian equipment such as stoves, collapsible furniture, working clothes, ceramics, utensils, etc. which were specifically conceived for the actual needs of an emergent, nomadic proletariat. Immediately after the Russian Revolution both Tatlin and Rodchenko were involved in teaching in the Moscow Vchutemas. Late in the 1920s Tatlin went to teach and work in Petrograd, and Rodchenko went to Inhuk where he organized the "artist-engineer" Constructivist group with which El Lissitzky was also to become associated. After this date all sorts of esthetic factions began to emerge in association with varying shades of political and technical opinion.

The architect Ladowsky initiated a typical splinter group during this period. His atelier propagated a school in which formal systems were to be generated partly out of utility and partly out of the principles of Gestalt psychology. His 1924 design for a suspended restaurant, in which a utilitarian expression of structure and movement is combined with a rhythmic progression of glazed prismatic volumes, is a polemical *tour de force* of composite invention—although hardly a rational solution to the problem of a restaurant. Although the Ladowsky group advocated an "objective" architecture, its end product was permeated by an ideal vocabulary of symbolic forms which were deemed to be expressive of typical psychic states such as "tranquility," "integrity," etc. It amounted, as Berthold Lubetkin has pointed out, to a universalism of a Larousse type which was in the last analysis highly subjective.[5]

El Lissitzky, architect, painter, photographer, propagandist, typographer and theoretician, was the synthetic artist *par excellence* of a cultural movement which was by definition synthetic. His "Proun" art work, its very name being a contracted compound of *Pro* and *Ounovis* (i.e., For a New Art), was in his own words seen as an *Umsteigestation* or "interchange station" from painting to architecture. Typical of such work is his famous Lenin Tribune project of 1920, which implied an architecture as equally synthetic of the whole visual environment as the Vesnin brothers' Pravda Building of 1923.

Lissitzky envisaged a world in which differences between various metiers were to be minimized to bring about the realm of the "artist-engineer." His versatile talent was able to produce a homogeneous spectrum of objects which, irrespective of their media, were created as essential complementary parts of a single socialist universe. Paradoxically enough his later non-metaphorical architectural projects appear subject to a greater degree of differentiation. His 1925 Wolkenbugel project, designed in association with Mart Stam, is a building entirely detached from the earth, which may account for its depiction as an object free from either kinetic or graphic elements. This is an avant-garde project even by today's standards where the past decade has seen proposals for similar structures by Kenzo Tange and Yona Friedman. Located at intersections along a concentric Moscow Boulevard, the Wolkenbugel were essentially propylaea, elevated high above the main thoroughfares leading to the city center and the Kremlin. As such they were to have been comparable as artifacts to Ledoux's Parisian *barrières*, while remaining the very antithesis of such monumentality. It is evident that Lissitzky recognized the radical nature of such a proposal, for he wrote of it in his book, *Russland*, 1929, as follows:

In comparison with the American skyscraper, the innovation here resides in the fact that the "utilized" space which is horizontal, is clearly separated from the services or support space which is vertical. . . . Externally we are presented with an entity in space which from all six directions is an elementarist diversity.[6]

The "Suprematist-Elementarist" vision of a dematerialized universe is embodied in Lissitzky's concept of imaginary space, wherein space becomes apparent solely by virtue of movement. This illusionistic creation of space through movement of either object or spectator seems to have implied for Lissitzky a corresponding dematerialization of form. From this stems Lissitzky's preoccupation with the suspension of structures clear of the earth of which he wrote in *Russland*: "Our idea for the future is to minimize the foundations that link to the earth. We have developed this idea already in a series of projects."[7] This was a reference not only to his own Wolkenbugel project, but more specifically to Ivan Leonidov's 1927 project for the Lenin Institute to be erected outside Moscow. With this competition entry for an institute of advanced study, Leonidov emerged into prominence from his obscure background as a painter and from his Vchutemas education and his study in the Vesnin atelier. His entire contribution was to be made within the next three years.

Leonidov was the last significant figure to emerge out of the milieu of the Russian architectural avant-garde prior to the advent of Stalinism. His output is to be distinguished from the more "utilitarian-objective" or, on occasion, more "formalistic" work of his immediate colleagues by virtue of its simplicity, elegance, delicacy and aura of unreality. Although it was not subject to a rigorous utilitarianism, it remained an architecture totally without rhetoric. This, combined with its intangible air of otherworldliness, now tends to project it more into our own foreseeable future than any other pioneer work of the same era. Leonidov shares with Lissitzky the honor of having anticipated much of our recent architectural avant-garde, as for instance the work of Wachsman, Le Ricolais, Buckminster Fuller, Friedman, Otto, Price, Malcolmson, etc.

Leonidov's Lenin Institute consisted of a library tower (15,000 books) and an elevated spherical auditorium (40,000 persons), plus a series of horizontal study buildings. The whole complex was designed for connection to the center city by an aerial railway. In 1927 its originality did not pass unrecognized. For Lissitzky it was "a physically dynamic architecture of floating volumes," while for the architect Ginzburg writing in 1927 its urban implications were clear. Guinzbourg wrote, "It dismisses traditional solutions and leads towards a new conception of urban space in which such a building would be able to find its place."[8]

Leonidov's conception of urban space was like that of Lissitzky, an "open city" or *"ville verte"* which transcended in actual formulation the then-current rival Soviet theories of "urbanism" and "disurbanism." Like Lissitzky, he was acutely aware that the urban structure of an unprecedented socialist mass society would automatically demand new "social condensers" for its effective organization. His 1927 Lenin Institute and his 1930 Cultural Palace/ Park are both attempts at formulating such "condensers." Simple prismatic glazed forms, suspension techniques and metallic geodesic construction are common elements in both projects. In each case the larger structures enclose unobstructed micro-environments, such as auditoriums, winter gardens, etc. These envelopes are climate-controlled and technically homogenous. Elevational manipulation is eschewed and reduced to the minimum. There is no attempt to borrow public "urban space use" conceptions from the past, such as the agora, etc. The approach is hedonistic, while remaining at the same time detached. The dirigible and its mooring mast are to be seen as pertaining to the same technical system as the earthbound structures. No plastic event occurs for the sake of local effect.

In 1930 Leonidov played a leading role in the OSA group's (i.e. Vesnin group's) design for the new town of Magnitogorsk. This plan was a development of Milutin's linear city concept, the town being designed as a continuous road settlement linking inland agriculture to the lakeside steel works. Leonidov's contribution is evident in the design of the housing sector and the layout of the cultural park on either side of the arterial road. The housing was arranged in unit clusters of eight "communes," each commune comprising 16 individual rooms arranged on two floors around a cruciform common area, divided into winter garden, lounge, gymnasiums and playcourts. Such a proposal offered a much more human form of the socialist settlement than the barrack-like high-rise communes, the super blocks then being generally postulated by Leonidov's contemporaries.

"The avant-garde, like any culture, can only flower in a climate where political liberty triumphs, even if it often assumes a hostile pose towards democratic and liberal society." So wrote Renato Poggioli in his book *The Theory of the Avant Garde*, recently published in English. Events occurring in Russia during the years 1930–32 certainly add support to this view, particularly the official party persecution of the architectural avant-garde in those years. Leonidov was one of many brilliant architects who were under personal attack from 1930 onwards. In 1932, the Soviet authorities foreclosed on all further cultural controversy and finally established "left classicism" as the official party line. From this dark night of history, the story and perhaps even the tradition of a lost avant-garde are now beginning to emerge.

1. For full text of program see *Gabo*, Harvard University Press, Cambridge, 1957, p. 153.

2. See "Futurism, Suprematism, Constructivism," by Camilla Gray, article in *Soviet Survey*.

3. *The Mind and Face of Bolshevism*, by Rene Fueloep-Miller, Harper Torchbook, New York, 1965, pp. 101-102.

4. *Russland; die Rekonstruktion der Architektur in der Sowjet-union*, by El Lissitzky, Vienna, 1930, p. 13.

5. See "The Builders" by Berthold Lubetkin, *Architectural Review*, May, 1932.

6. El Lissitzky, *op. cit.*, p. 30.

7. *Ville et Revolution*, by Anatole Kopp, Paris, 1967, p. 203.

8. El Lissitzky, *op. cit.*

New York Dada, 1910-30

by William Agee

William Agee has worked at the Archives of American Art, Detroit, was recently associate curator at the Whitney Museum, and is now with the Pasadena Museum of Art. He has published important documentary texts on the American Synchromist movement in Paris and on the work of Raymond Duchamp-Villon.

Discussion of the avant-garde in New York during the decade of 1910–20, when America first absorbed the radical innovations of modern art, has been devoted almost exclusively to Alfred Stieglitz and the artists who exhibited at his Gallery 291. Stieglitz' foresight, dedication and courage have deservedly earned him a place of fundamental importance, but the deference accorded him and his circle has resulted in an incomplete knowledge of a crucial period, for it has been identified as *the* single group to secure the advances of modern art in this country.

Another avant-garde circle existed concurrently with the 291 group, and although not unknown, it has not been sufficiently recognized as an authentic force in American art. From 1915 to 1923, however, the salon conducted by Walter Conrad Arensberg at his apartment on West 67th Street in New York was the source of many of the most far-reaching ideas injected into American art up to that time. It included Marcel Duchamp, Francis Picabia, Man Ray and a diverse group of Americans who together formed the center of Dada art in this country. Although their role in the Dada movement is well known, Duchamp, Picabia and Man Ray are usually considered European transients, alien to the American development. The extent to which Dada affected American modernism in these years, and the cohesiveness provided the movement by the Arensberg circle, has never been fully charted. By definition, an avant-garde lasts for a prescribed time only, losing its advanced status as its tenets become established conventions. But because we have overlooked its continuity and the extent of its influence, the Arensberg circle is in a real sense an historical rarity, an avant-garde which has remained largely separate and apart from our history. The purpose of this essay is thus to dwell more on the sources and extensions of Dada in America than on the well documented accomplishments of Duchamp, Man Ray and Picabia.

The comparative obscurity of the Arensberg circle can be traced not only to the long shadow cast by Stieglitz but to a misconception of Dada which has resulted in the general disrepute of the movement in the eyes of historians and artists alike. Dada has been viewed as nihilistic, espousing chaos, anarchy and the destruction of art, and therefore offering little if any positive achievement. However, it is now clear that in spite of itself Dada was responsible for a considerable body of unique work. Dada, in Arp's words, "sought to destroy the hoaxes of reason to discover an unreasoned order"; or as Tzara stated, "Dada tried to destroy, not so much art, as the idea one had of art, breaking down its rigid borders, lowering its imaginary heights—subjecting them to a dependence on man." Historians of the period in America have also assumed the existence of a single, homogeneous Dada style. But no stylistic definition can account for creations as disparate as Duchamp's Readymades, Picabia's machinist images or Schwitters' collages, and failing to find one, historians have for the most part neglected to follow the full course of the movement.

Furthermore, there has been a pervasive reluctance to consider American Dada during the first decades of modernism because the movement's revolutionary impulses, both social and esthetic, seem contrary to the American faith in "order," "logic" and "reason." Dada has been tacitly judged to be un-American; it has been a concept best avoided, which historians have frequently done—inevitably with absurd consequences. Artists themselves have been repelled by it, viewing it as an

aberration. Charles Burchfield, apparently caught in
the malaise following World War I, later said of his
work done after his discharge from the Army in
1919: "There followed a period of degeneracy in
my art that I have never been able to explain . . .
I later destroyed all the painting of this period . . .
viewed from any angle whatsover, there is not a
single redeeming feature about them—and I might
add that the vagaries of the Da-Da school were
nothing compared to mine at this time, though I had
never heard of Da-Daism then" (*Creative Art*, September, 1928).

Dada was officially christened in February, 1916,
at the Café Voltaire in Zurich, but with Duchamp
and Picabia here by mid-1915, New York shared
with Zurich and Paris in its nativity. That we should
turn away from a movement whose consequences
are still felt today seems implausible, all the more so
since Dada was the first movement born (even if in
a qualified sense) in this country. Traditionally
American artists have sought refuge in Europe for
training and inspiration. Synchromism, the first
American avant-garde movement, was founded in
Paris at the same time as Dada discovered here the
machine and the junk environment. Thereafter,
Dada was to touch American art—beyond Duchamp, Man Ray and Picabia—at diverse and unsuspected points.

Although the presence of three major Dadaists in
1915–17 offers strong evidence to the contrary, it

may be argued that at no single moment did New York sustain as intense an activity as any of the European centers. However, it would be wrong to conclude that Dada had only limited impact on American art. Even if New York Dada was less concentrated, its longevity surpassed that in the European capitals of the movement, where the focus shifted rapidly from city to city. The dates of New York Dada can be fixed from 1910, the moment of Benjamin de Casseres' first attacks on esthetic conventions, to 1930 when Arthur Dove did the last of his Dada-inspired collages. As Dada spread from Zurich to Berlin, then to Cologne and Hanover and finally to Paris, it was modified by the distinctly different character of each of the avant-garde groups within those cities. New York Dada on the other hand was unique in that it stayed almost completely within the domain of the Arensberg circle.

In its first stages, American Dada was initiated by a splinter group from the Stieglitz circle later absorbed into the Arensberg faction. De Casseres and Marius de Zayas, both of them close friends of Stieglitz and editors of his magazine *Camera Work*, were the first to launch a full-scale attack on the canons of art and morality and to define the attitudes later known as Dada. De Casseres' role has not passed unnoticed but he has never received due credit for the earliness and intensity of his assaults. In July, 1910, in *Camera Work*, he railed against the "sane and normal" in art and praised the "New

Dreamer" who "stands there revising all axioms." The next year in the October *Camera Work* he dwelt at some length on the creative powers submerged within the unconscious, forecasting the Dada concern for the irrational. In the January, 1912 issue, de Casseres had published a systematic disavowal of bourgeois rationalism:

In poetry, physics, practical life there is nothing . . . that is any longer moored to a certainty, nothing that is forbidden, nothing that cannot be stood on its head and glorified. . . .
Anarchy? No. It is the triumph of discrimination, the beatification of paradox, the sanctification of man by man. . . .
Nothing which lasts is of value . . . That which changes perpetually lives perpetually. . . .
I find my supremest joy in my estrangements. . . . I desire to become unfamiliar with myself. . . . I cling to nothing, stay with nothing, am used to nothing, hope for nothing. I am a perpetual minute.

In April, 1912, de Casseres explicitly invoked the Dada litany of revolt when he stated, "All great movements begin with the gesture of hate, of irony, of revenge. . . . There is a reevaluation going on in the art of the world today. There is a healthy mockery, a healthy anarchic spirit abroad. . . . No art is perfect until you have smashed it." As he pursued this tack from 1912 to 1915, he was joined by de Zayas, the Mexican writer and artist, who in the July, 1912, issue of *Camera Work* lamented the artist's loss of contact with the unknown, foreshadowing Dada's interest in the primitive by urging a new participation in the untrammeled instincts of the child's world. De Zayas concluded with the soon familiar Dada cry, "Art is dead," in which de Casseres concurred the next year.

When Picabia arrived in New York in January, 1913, to visit the Armory Show, his contacts with Duchamp had already made him discontented with the limits of art, yet it seems certain that contact with de Casseres and de Zayas quickened his pace of dissent. Upon arrival Picabia was immediately in touch with Stieglitz, meeting daily with him and the members of 291 until his return to Paris in April. The chant of de Casseres' "healthy anarchic spirit" echoes throughout Picabia's announcement (in the June, 1913, issue of *Camera Work*) of *"L'Ecole Amorphiste,"* the first Dada art manifestation to appear in this country. Picabia's manifesto included diagrams of two blank canvases entitled *Femme au Bain* and *La mer* and signed "Popaul Picador." By parodying these two standard academic themes, Picabia decisively renounced what he took to be the impoverished idealism of the West. His use of a pseudonym (as Duchamp was to adopt the female alias "Rrose Sélavy" in 1920) also established the Dada questioning of the relevance of personal identity to the work of art.

In turn, Picabia without doubt confirmed the diagnosis of social and creative ills proposed by de Zayas and de Casseres and may have encouraged de Zayas to extend his anti-art gestures. In a series of abstract caricatures hardly known today, de Zayas reduced portraits of public figures and members of the Stieglitz circle, including Picabia himself, to invented forms punctuated by mathematical equations. Like Picabia's blank diagrams, they repudiated the clichés of another tradition, the portrait "likeness." In its stead, de Zayas introduced a new symbolic-associative language which was a forerunner both of the Dadaists' formulae and numbers and of Picabia's object-portraits of 1915–17.

The exchange between Picabia and de Zayas, crucial to the embryonic stages of New York Dada, did not stop in the period between Picabia's return to Paris in April, 1913, and his second visit to New York in June, 1915. In the spring of 1914 de Zayas visited Picabia in Paris and may well have met Duchamp there. That fall, he brought back to New York numerous objects from Picabia's collection, many of which were exhibited at 291 in January, 1915. Picabia may have been partly responsible for the founding of the magazine 291 in March, 1915. Edited by de Zayas and Paul Haviland and published by Stieglitz in conjunction with his gallery, 291 was a continuing source of Dada art and ideas in all its 12 numbers, the last of which appeared in February, 1916. In it appeared some of Picabia's most famous Dada creations such as the sparkplug labeled *Portrait d'une jeune fille américaine dans l'état de nudité*. The publication of 291 was the last phase of the Dada activities of the Stieglitz circle.

Thereafter, everything revolved almost exclusively around those who gravitated to the Arensberg apartment.

Arensberg—poet, critic, patron, scholar of the Bacon-Shakespeare controversy—and his wife Louise were warm and congenial hosts. Arensberg was particularly receptive to all new ideas relating to the arts and enjoyed the company of those committed to such forms of expression. The nucleus of his circle consisted of Duchamp and Picabia and soon included Man Ray, who had met Duchamp shortly after the latter's arrival in May, 1915. The group soon attracted other lively artists, and by early 1916 the Arensberg apartment was the scene of endless activities and discussions carried on at all hours of the day and night. Until the Arensbergs moved to California in the early 1920s, their salon, one of the most extraordinary in our history, was visited by Albert Gleizes, Jean Crotti, Henri-Pierre Roché, Joseph Stella, Marsden Hartley, Katherine Dreier, Charles Demuth, Charles Sheeler, Arthur Dove, John Covert, Morton Schamberg, Walter Pach, John Sloan, George Bellows, Isadora Duncan, William Carlos Williams and Edgard Varèse. Under the stimulus of Duchamp and Picabia, most of the visitors were touched by Dada's radicalism. This center was also of inestimable value for the major works of art of the modernist revolution to be seen there. Arensberg's collection, one of the truly great holdings of modern art in this country, contained not only superb Picassos, Braques, Brancusis and Picabias, but the most comprehensive selection of Duchamps anywhere.

Unlike European Dada, the movement in this country was not equally literary and in fact produced very little writing. Its literary spokesman was Arensberg; he composed Dada poems and wrote the only American Dada manifesto. This virtually forgotten document was read in Paris in February, 1920, and published as part of "*Vingt-trois manifestes du mouvement dada*" in the May, 1920, issue of *Littérature*, the magazine published by Aragon, Soupault and Breton. In it Arensberg claimed that Dada belonged to America as well as to the world. His role as spokesman also included considerable support of the three Dada magazines which appeared in New York: two issues (April and May, 1917) of *The Blind Man*; a single issue of *Rongwrong* (May, 1917) and one issue of *New York Dada* (1921).

The catalytic force behind the Arensberg circle and indeed all Dada was Marcel Duchamp, who, by the time of his arrival in New York, had reversed nearly every accepted law of painting. It was in New York that he executed the plans for his masterpiece, *The Bride Stripped Bare by Her Bachelors, Even*, an enigmatic compendium of mechanical images which negates the possibility of any ultimate meaning of human union and hence life itself. In 1918, while still in New York, Duchamp executed his last painting, *Tu m'*, a sprawling collection of painted shadows of his Readymades and such real objects as a safety pin and bottle brush in which the tangible and immaterial appear interchangeable. In New York Duchamp also produced many Readymades; intentionally devoid of esthetic interest, they subverted by acts of sheer will the foundations of the artist's role. Finally, in 1920, a year before returning to Paris, Duchamp rejected the role of artist altogether for that of "engineer."

Duchamp's presence in New York also afforded American artists the opportunity to witness public acts of anti-social, anti-art nature which could not help but expand their sense of the artist as a social critic. His submission of the notorious urinal signed "R. Mutt" to the 1917 Society of Independent Artists —founded that year by members of the Arensberg group, among them Duchamp himself, as an open, jury-free exhibition—exposed even the most liberal thought when the "fountain" was predictably rejected. Duchamp continued to disrupt the Society's activities; he arranged for a lecture to be given by Arthur Cravan at the exhibition hall, clearly hoping for a repeat of Cravan's performance in Paris in 1914 when he had fired several pistol shots. Duchamp was not disappointed. Cravan arrived dead drunk and began undressing; he was finally subdued and carried away by the police. Duchamp commented that it had been a wonderful lecture.

Duchamp's unique methods were less easily understood than those of Picabia, who as a consequence exerted a more readily available influence on American art. While in New York during his second stay in 1915–17, Picabia discovered the expressive potential of the machine. His view of the machine as an extension of human thought and feeling presented an entirely new range of formal and symbolic properties which immediately affected several American artists. One aspect of Picabia's machinist style—composite invented images making schematic diagrams—figured in his renewal of collaboration with de Zayas. Picabia's *Voilà Elle* and de Zayas' *Elle*, which appeared as a two-page spread in the November, 1915, issue of *291*, represented a new attack on mindless and unfeeling feminine passion. From Picabia's assemblage of various machine parts, de Zayas adapted a similar diagrammatic arrangement of words and phrases which echoed the compositional outlines of *Voilà Elle*. It is worth noting that this collaboration continued with de Zayas' frequent contributions to Picabia's magazine *391*, published in Barcelona, New York, Zurich and Paris from 1917 to 1924.

Man Ray, the first American artist to join the Dada ranks, was decisively influenced by Duchamp. Prior to their meeting in 1915, Man Ray had been painting in a modified Cubist vein but by 1916 in *The Rope Dancer Accompanies Herself with Her Shadows*, his work reflected Duchamp's long interest in movement and states of change. Thereafter, Man Ray furthered the Dada rejection of conventional techniques with his development of mechanical methods and creation of objects uniting disparate non-art materials in unexpected associations. In 1918 he did his first aerographs, using a spray-gun and stencil, the year after he had created his Rayographs by means of directly exposing to light sensitized paper on which were placed various objects. Moreover, Man Ray affirmed in such assembled objects as *The Enigma of Isidore Ducasse* the prerogative of art to be completely private and self-referential, recording the most obscure stirrings of the unconscious. Before leaving for Paris in 1921 he was active in the Arensberg circle and, as a close friend of Duchamp, helped him edit the one issue of *New York Dada*.

Duchamp, Picabia and Man Ray were the three major Dada pioneers in New York, but the movement was by no means confined to them. Jean Crotti, Duchamp's brother-in-law, was in New York in 1915–17 and was a regular visitor to the Arensberg apartment. Following Duchamp's lead in the *Large Glass*, Crotti did several paintings on glass; more specifically Dadaist was his portrait of Duchamp (now destroyed) made from a wire coathanger, false optician's eyes and a mass of wire hair. Crotti also worked in a machinist style indebted to Picabia.

The first American after Man Ray to produce work directly indebted to Dada was Morton L. Schamberg, a finer artist than has been supposed, whose premature death in 1918 severed a promising career. He painted in a Cubist and Orphic-Synchromist manner until 1916 when his close friend Charles Sheeler introduced him to Duchamp, Picabia and others of the Arensberg circle. Picabia's machinist paintings—shown at de Zayas' Modern Gallery in January, 1916—made an immediate impression on Schamberg, and by the end of that year he had evolved his own fluent mechanical expressions. Their originality is a tribute to Schamberg's powers since they fall into three phases which parallel the development of Picabia's machinist style almost verbatim. *Camera Flashlight* (Collection Dr. and Mrs. Ira Leo Schamberg, Jenkintown, Pa.), for instance, recalls Picabia's object-portraits, particularly *Ici, C'est Ici Stieglitz* (Metropolitan Museum) of 1915 in which a camera represents Stieglitz. Both artists found a source in Paul Haviland's statement, published in *Camera Work*, Sept.-Oct., 1915, which embodied their feelings for the machine: "Man made the machine in his own image. She has limbs which act; lungs which breathe; a heart which beats; a nervous system through which runs electricity. The phonograph is the image of the voice; the camera is the image of his eye. . . ." Schamberg's camera is more abstract and painterly than Picabia's, but his image of the eye is far more literal in its resemblance to a flash attachment.

Such Schamberg paintings as *Composition*, 1916 (Columbus Gallery of Fine Arts, Columbus, Ohio), with its diagrammatic use of machine parts, relate to a second phase of Picabia's machinist style, which reduces machines to highly simplified abstract compositions like that of *Fantasie*, 1915 (published in *291*, #10-11, December, 1915–January, 1916).

Schamberg's best-known abstractions, like the 1916 *Mechanical Abstraction*, rendered with a spare and precise linearity, were indebted to Picabia's imaginative machines of *Voilà Elle* and *Machine tournez vite*, ca. 1916–17 (Galleria Schwarz, Milan). In a third phase Picabia developed a stylistic subdivision of more painterly, brushed and richly colored elements in works like *Voilà la femme* (Collection Robert Lebel, Paris) which were subsequently paraphrased by Schamberg in his *Untitled: Mechanical Abstraction* (Collection Mrs. Jean Loeb Whitehill, New York). Schamberg modified Picabia's machinist style by deleting subtitles and inscriptions and by paying greater attention to a meticulous execution, finish and polish. Yet this should not cloud his Dada origins. Should we be tempted to forget Schamberg's allegiance to the Dada order of revolution, we need only consider his plumbing construction irreverently called *God*, ca. 1917–18, as nice a Dada blasphemy as any. Here again he was indebted to Picabia, who had subtitled *Fantasie*, "Man created God in his image." Given this inscription, and Haviland's statements, "Man made the machine in his own image," Schamberg's equation of God and an ordinary mechanical part is easily understood. Schamberg was assisted in the construction of *God* by Baroness Elsa von Freytag von Loringhoven, an eccentric poetess who made Dada artifacts and reliefs from bits of colored rubbish and tinfoil. She was herself a Dada personification, habitually shav-

141

ing her head and painting it purple, dressing in an old Mexican blanket and wearing an inverted coal scuttle for a hat, a vegetable grater as a brooch and long ice-cream spoons for earrings.

Picabia's discovery of American machinery alerted artists in this country to a native iconography previously considered unworthy. To be sure, by 1914 Marin, Weber and Stella, like the Futurists, had interpreted the sensations and kaleidoscope rhythms of the modern urban world. But the machine itself, conceived as an independent, self-contained object, isolated from its urban environment and rendered with literal clarity, only found its way into American art through Duchamp and Picabia. Its assimilation, first through Schamberg and certain works by Man Ray, was to provide in the 1920s and '30s an important source of Precisionism. This movement, although like Dada ultimately indebted to Cubism for its formal syntax, made recurring stylistic and thematic references to the machinist idiom of 1915–1918. Charles Sheeler, Joseph Stella and Charles Demuth were among those who, after Schamberg, elaborated the clean, sharp edges of the Precisionist vocabulary. It is no coincidence that all three were virtually charter members of the Arensberg circle, close friends of Duchamp and well aware of Picabia's machinist paintings.

Until he saw Picabia's new paintings in 1915, Joseph Stella had been working in an orthodox Futurist manner which interpreted the carnival life of the city in interlacing fragments of color. Thereafter Stella introduced a new realism while focusing on single industrial and urban monuments, isolated as objects in much the same way as Picabia's machines. His *Factories* (Museum of Modern Art), 1918, loom as imaginative and colossal machines, more like a giant blow-up of a Picabia than either his earlier Futurist paintings or views of directly observed American industry. After 1918 Stella resumed his more overtly Futurist style but even when he deals with famous landmarks such as the *Brooklyn Bridge* (Yale University), 1919–20, one senses his awareness of the monument as a huge and efficient machine.

To a great extent the Precisionist themes of Sheeler and Demuth were rural and architectural, portraying an older and more tranquil America. Nevertheless, in such paintings as the 1917 *White Architecture* (William H. Lane Foundation, Leominster, Mass.), ostensibly based on a clapboard building, Demuth introduced mechanical overtones in the piston-like spire. Demuth also appropriated the formal device first employed by Picabia and Schamberg of centering the image within the empty edges of the canvas to emphasize a smoothly functioning internal structure.

Some of Demuth's finest paintings, however, incorporate specifically machinist imagery. *Machinery* (Metropolitan Museum), 1920, and *Paquebot Paris* (Columbus Gallery of Fine Arts, Columbus, Ohio),

1921-22, include recognizable industrial parts and are, like Stella's paintings, magnified to an American scale. Though their ultimate source is in Picabia, such high points of Precisionism as Demuth's *My Egypt* (Whitney Museum), 1927, with its realistic, towering American grain elevator, transform Picabia's intimate sense of scale. Demuth also adapted other Dada phases of Picabia's work such as the object-portraits of 1915. Charles Demuth's *Poster Portrait* of Georgia O'Keeffe, 1924, represented the painter Georgia O'Keeffe as a plant symbolizing the natural forms which were her hallmark, just as Picabia had summarized her husband, Stieglitz, as a camera.

Although the sharp-focus realism of Charles Sheeler as well as his belated use of industrial imagery seems to remove him from any consideration of the machinist style, a careful examination of his evolution reveals his debt to Picabia and Duchamp. After referring to certain passages of Picabia's 1913 *Udnie* (Musée National d'Art Moderne, Paris) in his abstract *Flower Forms* (Mrs. Earle Horter, Philadelphia), Sheeler gradually modified his fragmented Cubist planes until by 1923 he had reached an immaculate naturalism. For several years thereafter he concentrated almost exclusively on architecture, botany and interiors, but in 1929 he translated the mechanical equipment of a boat's superstructure in *Upper Deck* (Fogg Museum, Harvard), a more realistic version of a theme recalling Demuth's *Paquebot Paris*. If Sheeler's experience of the industrial-mechanical world was tardy, it was deeply committed, and he soon expanded it into images of mammoth industrial complexes such as the 1934 *City Interior* (Worcester Museum). More than any of the other Precisionists, Sheeler transformed the machine into a specifically American subject, yet one still hears the distant Dada echoes. That the formative experience of the original machinist style was never far from Sheeler's memory was evident as late as 1952 in his *Meta-Mold* (Mrs. Otto Spaeth, New York), a painting whose gears and wheels pay homage to Duchamp's *Malic Molds* of 1914–15 (Mrs. Marcel Duchamp, New York) and Picabia's *Réveil-Matin* (Galleria Schwartz, Milan), 1919. Sheeler like Demuth, also touched on other aspects of Dada. In his *Self-Portrait*, 1923, he presented what might be taken as his true self—his voice—in the form of a telephone, while his material figure appears only as a dim, intangible shadow.

Gerald Murphy, an expatriate whose brief career as an artist is usually associated with Léger, also found in the machinist style a rich fund of pictorial invention. His painting of 1923, *Watch*, is another example of American amplification of intimate scale into an entire construction of intermeshed flywheels, again indebted to Picabia's *Réveil-Matin*. Murphy expanded this machinist complex into the more robust pistons and shafts of *Engine Room* (Mrs. Gerald Murphy) which he executed, like the Precisionists, with an American objectivity and meticulous surface finish.

An artist of considerable if brief accomplishment who is barely mentioned in our histories, John Covert, experienced the Dada influence differently. After returning from Europe in 1914, Covert was introduced to Duchamp by his cousin, Walter Arensberg, and became a regular visitor to the apartment on West 67th Street. Covert was among those who helped to organize the Society of Independent Artists and he served as its first director. His active association with the members of the Arensberg circle was reflected in his painting by 1919, when he abandoned pure abstractions and began to incorporate Dada principles. In *Brass Band* (Yale University) of that year Covert defined the planes and spatial direction by attaching string cords directly to the composition board as Duchamp had attached wire to the glass panes of *The Bride Stripped Bare by Her Bachelors, Even.* These tentative Dada anti-art gestures were intensified the same year in *Vocalization,* in which Covert more flagrantly mocked the "pure" planes of Cubist abstraction by gluing wooden dowels to the surface in much the same way that Picabia had used macaroni in *Le Midi* (Yale University), 1917. Covert's most fertile and inventive embodiment of Dada was *Time,* also 1919, in which he employed upholstery tacks interspersed with equations and mathematical drawings to create surface divisions that rejected traditional techniques. In 1923 Covert, like Murphy, concluded his career to return to business.

While she is best known as a collector and patron, Katherine Dreier was also a painter whose work reflected the innovations of Duchamp and Picabia. Deeply impressed by the Armory Show, she began a study of modern art which led to a long and close friendship with Duchamp, through whom she was exposed to Picabia. Her 1918 *Abstract Portrait of Marcel Duchamp*, like Picabia's *Portrait of Marie Laurencin* (Mrs. Harry Lewis Winston), ca. 1916–1917, reduced portraiture to a series of mechanical elements and conveyed her sense of Duchamp's energy and intellect.

By 1920, Katherine Dreier had assembled a collection which rivaled Arensberg's in richness and depth. It was particularly representative of New York Dada and could count among its resources major works by Duchamp, Man Ray, Picabia, Max Ernst and later Kurt Schwitters. Miss Dreier's commitment to modern art had convinced her of the value of and need for an organization devoted to educating the public in its principles. She enlisted the aid of Duchamp and Man Ray and in 1920 the Société Anonyme, the first museum of modern art, was founded. Galleries were opened on 47th Street and a regular exhibition program began in the spring of that year, supplemented by an extensive series of lectures by artists. In its first three years the Société Anonyme was a hotbed of Dada ideas and activities and was particularly important in maintaining the movement after Duchamp and Man

147

Ray had left for Paris in 1921. Joseph Stella was also active on its committees, and the first exhibitions regularly included work by Picabia, Duchamp, Man Ray, Schamberg and Stella. Part of the First International Dada Fair, held in Berlin in June, 1920, was to have been brought to its gallery, but the plans never materialized. On April 1, 1921, the Société sponsored a symposium on Dada. It is difficult to gauge the precise extent to which these activities encouraged Dada in New York, but the fact remains that they coincided with a new flourish of the movement.

In November, 1920, and March, 1921, Société Anonyme exhibitions included the collages of Kurt Schwitters, the first occasions on which his work was shown in this country. These collages, which Schwitters distinguished from other Dada by his term Merz, were a primary example of the desire to abolish art as a remote discipline and reunite it with life. The scraps of paper and discarded tickets which among other cast-off and derelict momentos constituted the Merz collages recreated an entire autobiographical world. After they were shown in New York, Schwitters quickly became a Dada influence in America as important as Duchamp or Picabia.

Joseph Stella responded to the Merz collages with a series of his own which must be considered among the finest Dada-inspired work done in this country. The components of Stella's collages are even more ordinary and pulverized than Schwitters'. In perhaps his most audacious one, *Chiclets*, Stella arranged three mutilated and stained gum wrappers in a vertical composition with all the presence of a pure abstraction. The tiny head of *The Bookman*, ca. 1921, was created from cigarette papers; he parodied his Futurist paintings by tilting pieces of newsprint in the *Study for Skyscraper* (published with *The Bookman* in *The Little Review*, Autumn, 1922). In executing about three-dozen collages from the early '20s into the '30s, Stella worked with disparate fragments of matchbooks, leaves, theater programs and totally empty, bleached paper.

Schwitters like Duchamp and Picabia was liberating for Stuart Davis. Although not a member of the Arensberg circle, Davis kept his studio in the building next to Duchamp's and came to know him as well as Picabia and Man Ray. Characterizing them as a group Davis said they "couldn't help broadcasting revolution wherever they went." Duchamp's "fountain," submitted to the 1917 Independents, worked like a "time bomb" in Davis' consciousness: "Duchamp's suggestion worked slowly. Unesthetic material, absurd material, non-arty material—ten years later I could take a worthless eggbeater, and the change to a new association would inspire me," (quoted in Rudi Blesh, *Stuart Davis*, N.Y., 1960). There is evidence, however, that Dada had a more immediate effect: Davis had acknowledged that Picabia's macaroni and feather in *Le Midi* made it easier for him to "sew buttons and glue excelsior on the canvas without feeling any sense of guilt," and in fact Davis had incorporated collage elements in his 1921 *Itlksez* to create a stick figure inscribed with a Dada nonsense word. Like Picabia's *Match Woman* (Collection Mme. Simone Collinet, Paris), Davis' stick figure is an implicit Dada rejection of Western figurative painting. In 1921—the year the Société Anonyme sparked a new phase of Dada—Davis produced several paintings such as *Cigarette Papers* which emulated the discarded, anti-art materials used by Schwitters and Stella. Davis cleaned up these materials and presented them as pure elements of art, as Schamberg and others had refined earlier Dada art, but there can be no escaping the ultimate source.

Although his work shows no overt evidence of Dada, Marsden Hartley, possessed of an inquisitive and venturesome intellect, caught the spirit of the Dada proclamations of freedom. Hartley had called regularly at the Arensberg apartment and was an active participant in the Société Anonyme's lecture and exhibition program. In his book *Adventures in the Arts*, 1921, he included a chapter titled "The Importance of Being Dada" which perhaps best summarizes the non-doctrinaire, non-political nature of American Dada. Hartley embraced Dada for re-uniting art and life and for restoring to art the free and unbridled expression of the individual.

Perhaps stimulated by the activities of the Société Anonyme, Holger Cahill was prompted in about 1921 to found a movement called Inje-Inje which closely resembled Dada, even to the childlike syllables of its name. Cahill had learned that Inje was the only word in the language of a tribe of South American Indians who communicated through a wide range of inflections and gestures. Paralleling the Dada exploration of the primitive, Cahill hoped to return art to a state of simplicity and direct expression. Painting was thus to be reduced to horizontal and vertical lines. He also planned concerts of primitive music in conjunction with the movement, but like most of the program these plans were unfulfilled. During its brief existence of two or three years, Inje-Inje attracted such artists as Mark Tobey, Alfred Maurer and John Sloan.

The most blatant example of the prevalent historical prejudice against Dada in American art involves the collages and reliefs Arthur Dove executed between 1924 and 1930. They are pure Dada in conception and technique, yet hardly a word about Dada can be found in the Dove literature, which is never at a loss to attribute the collages to such sources as nineteenth-century Americana. The evidence is, however, irrefutable. Dove had visited the Arensberg circle and was certainly aware of Dada developments. One link between his initial contact with Dada and his collages is a painting of 1922 titled *Gear* (ex-coll. Edith Halpert); picturing two shafts merged with a wheel, it is directly related to Picabia's machinist style.

The catalyst for Dove's collages, however, was

another phase of Schwitters' work—his relief constructions. While Dove's 1925 *Portrait of Alfred Stieglitz* obviously recalls Picabia's symbolic representation of Stieglitz as a camera, its assemblage of separate elements including a camera lens and photographic plate is closer to Schwitters' constructions. Even closer to Schwitters' old junk are the magnifying glass, chicken bone and scale combined in *The Intellectual*, also 1925, as a Dada mockery of the limits of reason. Dove found as wide an expressive range in his collages as did Stella. Some verged on total abstraction, like *Monkey Fur*, 1928, where the only discernible image is the vestige of a head amid fur, tinfoil and rusted metal. In her book *Modern Art*, 1926, Katherine Dreier referred to Dove as the "only American Dadaist." An overstatement, to be sure, but a revealing, contemporary account of a relationship we have overlooked ever since.

Dada in America, then, was more than a passing European phenomenon limited to Duchamp, Man Ray and Picabia. American Dada had its own distinctive traits and inflections, just as Dada varied between Zurich and Berlin or Hanover and Paris. Duchamp, Picabia and Man Ray were the major figures, but to limit the consideration of New York Dada to them is to miss a considerable body of American art. Much of it represents brief, erratic and unsure episodes, but to a great extent that is the pattern of all early modernism in this country. Together, however, those episodes constitute a significant phase in our history. They are part of a mosaic that must be pieced together if we are to understand the past that continues to shape our present.

Gotham News, 1945-60

by Louis Finkelstein

Louis Finkelstein is head of the art department at
Queens College and a painter. He has written numerous
articles on the New York School.

WHAT any avant-garde is, was or could have been is never actually to be known. The problem is not wholly in the phenomenon but in the knowing. As in the case of the little particles in the physicists' big expensive acceleration whizbangs, the very act of measuring alters the nature of the data. When events recede into history they become a matter of dates and documents, interpretation and speculation. For the avant-garde of the '40s and '50s in New York, which came to be known as Abstract-Expressionism, there were many and varied accounts of what it was and where it was going even while the events were unfolding. What follows is not a description of its historical development, but rather a partisan, personal view, presenting a theoretical rationale of the essential unity of Abstract-Expressionism with particular regard to its avant-garde status.[1]

It is just this matter of essential unity which was at issue in discussions at the artists' Club, discussions which were completely hostile to any kind of theoretical formulation and which instead seemed to cultivate a wide range of disagreement. The first attempt to denote any coherent movement was under the name of "Intrasubjectivism," and later when the term "Abstract-Expressionism" became current, many artists resisted its application to themselves. (Later on it became a label of commercial value as in the assertion of one dealer, "If it's Abstract-Expressionism we know it's good.") Beyond the simple matter of a name, two major formulations were advanced during the period, systems of judgment around which ideas tended to coalesce, advocated by Clement Greenberg and Harold Rosenberg, and apparently diametrically opposed.

For Greenberg the essential characteristics were formal, involving a transformation of pictorial space in terms of the patent surface elements on the canvas, and were part of the whole history of Western art from the Renaissance on, conceived of as formal evolution: in short Abstract-Expressionism was a style like other styles, with achievable standards of structural completeness. For Rosenberg, on the other hand, the essence of Abstract-Expressionism resided in its breaking with the very idea of style: in the life style of the artist as a continuing revolutionist assuming precedence over the qualities of the painting, in the rejection of formal completeness or even coherence as an aim, in the valuation of the action which the artist engaged in as against the created result. The creative process was an act of destruction of the past, even the artist's own immediate past.

Each of these representations was highly authoritative since they were both based in large measure upon the utterances of the artists involved directly to their authors. Each formulation was roundly objected to by many of the artists to whom it was supposed to apply and each was avidly snatched up by numerous epigones as a sure guide to currency and success. Exemplary of the two divergent positions, if not directly derived, were the programs and practices of a succeeding generation (or, by now, two) of artists, the formalist line extending to the various ramifications of Post-Painterly Abstraction, including staining, Minimalism, object making, Color-Field painting and Op, while the revolutionist anti-esthetic stance was projected in Happenings, mixed mediums, Pop and eventually in a new coloring to the techniques of social and political protest, i.e. it ceased to function in art so much as (often literally) in the streets.

For the events each was attempting to explain, both the Greenberg view and the Rosenberg view remain glittering half-truths. It was not simply a stock avant-gardist negation or programmatic anti-intellectualism which led artists to deny the validity of these views so much as the fact that each assertion tended to deny and miscomprehend what was true of the other in a way which left their conflicting claims and possible intersection unexplicated. While events were yet novel and in the center of the stage it was perhaps permissible to hold that for a work of art to be good it had to be new, although whether such an assertion was meant to be prescriptive or descriptive is not clear. Beyond its initial appearance the work of art becomes, at the hands of the historians, curators, critics, dealers and collectors, a member of a stylistic category. Documentation and the description of types and market values replace the esthetic experience of individual works. Recently Greenberg has responded to this situation by asserting that esthetic experience is properly only that of the first instance of confrontation, before category, reflection and critical exposition intervene. One understands what he means and the idea is well taken, up to a point. The effect of his argument is to restrict esthetic discourse to the purely visual properties of the object. This limitation in respect to Abstract-Expressionism is Procrustean in that the principal avant-garde property of Abstract-Expressionism, which is to say before it became a style and a commodity, was to propose to be more than its patent formal elements. Latterly emergent and serving to define this more sharply are contrary assertions by Frank Stella, Donald Judd and others that the work of art refers and consists of only what is actually *there*, in the object. The real radicalism of the Abstract-Expressionist proposal was to open up the modalities of relation between the physical form of the picture and the reality to which it refers. Rather than depict the objects of experience, Abstract-Expressionism sought to render a veridical account of the quality of experience itself. For the same reason, and with the same ultimate appeal to truthfulness to life as in Joyce, this involved new forms; but, as in Joyce it was not undertaken for the satisfaction of purely stylistic ends.

The ambiguities, not only between formal and expressive aims such as underlie the Rosenberg-Greenberg face-off, but also as to the ways the work of art refers to experience, arise neither from art nor from the processes of art, but from the nature of experience itself. In Surrealist multiple imagery we understand the puns, displacements, metaphors, dream symbols, transformations and juxtapositions because in large measure they are clearly illustrated as such. For example, in the works of Matta, despite his technical inventions and concern for what he calls non-Euclidean space, what we sense is an accurate portrayal of an unusual set of circumstances rather than a transformation of portrayal itself. It is this implication of literalness which gives his work a science-fiction quality. In Abstract-Expressionism, quite the reverse: it is the modes of reference which are open and strange rather than the things referred to.

A good example of this kind of polyreferentialness is to be found in the oeuvre of Joan Mitchell, who, while one of the younger, and therefore not strictly pioneer, members of the movement, has had a continuing high level of achievement. Virtually all of her paintings are in some sense landscapes. Yet in what sense? Are they organizations of spatial relations such as are found in landscape, a set of symbols of landscape elements and of themes associated with landscape, a recall of retinal impressions derived from landscape, the species of distribution of focus and unfocus, of closed and opened, of weighted and unweighted, or in and out; are they the rhythms of landscape or of body and eye movements while in landscape; are they calligraphic play involving an analogy of brushstrokes to natural forms; are they the recall of specific landscape or of the modes of transformation of landscape into art; or are they indeed all of these and perhaps more?

In each and every Abstract-Expressionist work such issues of transformation are up for grabs. Moreover it seems of particular importance that the categories of interpretation seem to shift in the course of our looking at the picture, so that we are never left with the clear support for just one reading. Thus we can never see it as an esthetic whole, never the patent form, as in a Stella, but rather the sum of possible suggestions, of re-presentations of its presentational form. Such will be the case in any number of de Koonings, particularly those from around 1958 and 1959 which are generally called "landscapes" since some of them have landscape titles. We see the flat marks on the plane. It is not a dream space we see along the lines formulated by Robert Goldwater in his *Space and Dream* catalogue (Knoedler, 1967), but, based on the precedents for spatial reading in many de Koonings, both earlier and later, neither are the paintings flat. The observer can scarcely decide the distance between brushstrokes and this will vary depending on what is read as light, as gesture, as bulk, as void. In Guston's *The Painter's City* it is not a view of a city from the outside, the shapes of the city from the inside, buildings, people hurrying in the street, the feeling of being in the city, the idea of a city, a dream or a romance of the city, the tatteredness, the dirtiness, the elegance, the charm—but all of these. In fact, from conversations with Guston, I am quite sure that whatever I see he will call it something else, and yet I will be right too. This polyreferential quality was everywhere—Motherwell's "Spanish" paintings (about the accuracy of which he was to have a dispute with Vicente), in the visionary implications of Still and Rothko, in the denotative shifts of space, mass and movement in Kline and Brooks.

It was just this refusal to reject any possibilities of construction which infuriated Ad Reinhardt and made him the constant critic of his contemporaries as well as a hero and prophet of the purportedly closed-off art-as-art which followed. In one sense Ad was right. After everybody's eyes became accustomed to Abstract-Expressionism's violence, and in the course of its becoming assimilated into the museums, i.e. as it ceased to be avant-garde in the sense of novel, Abstract-Expressionist works became greatly admired for their paint quality, for their formal invention, for their holding the surface. And the assertions of the artists regarding subjective intensity became viewed as a kind of self-indulgent slop, off the point and tolerable only as a pretext to arrive at the creation of beauty. Indeed at the last big Pollock show at the Modern Museum (1967) it was the impression of consummate elegance rather than Expressionist anguish which seemed to prevail.

What is essential to the understanding of Abstract-Expressionism in its specifically avant-gardist aspect, as opposed to what may be eventually seen as a temporary and historically conditioned reaction to it, is to examine further its proposal (which has been for the moment thrust aside) to stand for experience in a new and more accurate way and to appeal to the standards of experience rather than to those of art. Here some speculative recourse must be made to the study of perception on both physiological and psychological levels. While some efforts have been made to interpret artistic phenomena psychologically on both psychoanalytic and Gestaltist lines, the results have not yet been particularly fruitful. Relatively recent formulations, however, are suggestive in casting new light on the problem, and much of the previous difficulty may be the result of inadequate estimates of the nature of experience itself.

Contrary to the conventional view, seeing is neither a fixed physiological process nor a fixed disclosure of characteristics of objects or spatial relations. Our brains do not replicate patterns physically corresponding to the specific formal characteristics of what is perceived, nor assign them necessarily fixed synaptic connections, as has been held by Gestaltist and associationist views respectively. Any instance of perception is the occasion of a kinetic series of electrical discharges of wide variability as to sequence, location and interconnection. The specific dynamic characteristics of timing and rhythm are of as much consequence as the synaptic connections involved. Neither the number of events in terms of spatio-temporal patterns nor their import appears to be clearly limitable. How such dynamic events produce meaning or recognition is not at all clear. It is clear, however, on the basis of experimental evidence, that the constructions made by the perceiver in the course of sensation are subject to a great degree of variability and are dependent on such factors as prior clues, anticipatory set and the past experience as well as present purposes of the individual. We do not see a thing as it is, but as a such-and-such, precisely as we perceive an abstract picture under certain and often variable modalities, that is within a given subjective form which is actively projected by the perceiver as a personal transaction with the material. Interpretation and association are not subsequent to perception, but enable us to order our perceptions at all.

At this point the scientist restricts himself to facts, which at the present time are still of a relatively trivial nature, where the artist permits himself a leap. I suggest that each event within the brain in the course of perception, which may be thought of as the unfolding of a pattern or of an intersection of patterns, is the occasion of a general form, which I shall call an Idea. The general form is completely unlike the discrete storage unit in a computer in that it has a potential for multiple specification. This Idea could comprehend at one and the same time a shape or a family of shapes, sounds, colors, words, emotions, whole objects of experience, like persons or places, all simultaneously available for further codification through an immediately sequent scanning process which reduces the potentials into particular levels of concresence by sensuous reinforcement and redirection.

Synesthesia, or the spontaneous combining of sense images, is a characteristic of memory experts and children and is replaced in most people in varying degrees by ratiocinative thought. Synesthesia also provides the model for our interpretation of one component of esthetic events. Commonly, esthetic experience is identified with the realization of harmony or order. For those systems which are formalist in predilection, this identification suffices to characterize the whole nature of the experience. In recent years this notion has been employed by

Greenberg (and others) as the basis of a series of self-fulfilling prophecies. That is, he, Greenberg, has lauded works which restrict themselves to "purely esthetic" properties, and then cited the artists that he has propelled into prominence for this reason as evidence of this artistic groundswell. There is, however, another component in esthetic events, one which is peculiarly difficult to grasp for both academics and businessmen—unless they are provided with some sort of useful handles, such as iconography or the topical appeal of a certain kind of subject matter—and that is meaning delivered through the form. I am speaking of the extra import, beyond what is given in the subject, sometimes associated with mystical visions, sometimes with drug-induced hallucinations, sometimes given in natural states of exaltation, but also what the artist experiences when he is creating, and the spectator, when he is with it. This arises from the natural order of the brain which, in this definition of esthetic as the intersection of the formal and the signifying, is inherently esthetic. It is not only in the actively polyreferential character of our experience, as shown in synesthesia, that the poetic faculty of the brain resides, but also in its marvelous range of association, retrieval and pattern recognition, which completely differentiates it from the computer.

What the computer does not do is see. I am not talking of that kind of seeing which is programmed to read numbers on bank checks, but that apparently unstructured, openly anticipant seeing which is part of the continuity of an organism. Consequently the machine is not free to construct meanings. Our assumptions of meaning are the result of our operation with the real world and it is here that our notions of meaning are stored. That is we assume the world to be continuous with itself, tied into a connected set of consequences. When we understand coherence it is the coherence we have already encountered. We individuate, we place its consequences into new constellations by tying it together with recognitions of our transactions with it, i.e., what is happening to us. In ordinary seeing the potentials for meaning are sharply reduced by each functional activity we are engaged in. Likewise our sense of any larger unity, any coherence to our total existence, is thrust aside into series of disparate events, few of which meaningfully define each other.

Esthetic experience, visual or otherwise, is the opposite. We attribute a forceful emotional content to a sensation or the object of sensation exactly by widening and activating a range of reference and significance beyond either functional demands or the supposedly patent characteristics of the display. This is the contrary of the formalist tenet that we are moved by forms in themselves. Further, if we do not in some way unify what is being experienced by building it into a deliberately made structure and interdependence in excess of that which is usually manifest in our various and disparate relations with life, it remains only a flux of feeling, a mood or a fantasy, and recedes back into the indistinguishability of mere things. The kinds of unity which were constructable prior to Abstract-Expressionism were relatively simplistic, culture-bound to some closed set of deterministically referenced connotations, for Cubism and Surrealism as well as for older styles—i.e., they had a certain sort of literalness toward a fixity which experience itself did not possess.

In painting, the interesting consideration is the interplay between the characteristics of the image and the technical and physical properties of the picture to arrive at a situation approximating, in its power to involve the beholder, the power of the subjective form of experience. Here both Cubism and Surrealism provided clues to the displacement of the usual relations between subject-matter and form. An example of what I mean is furnished by Pollock's *Pasiphae*, which could not have arrived at its formal or thematic proposals without the stereotypes provided by these two schools. It belongs to a class of works which includes various Picasso rapes, lady matadors and tauromachies as well as Matta's *Vertigo of Eros*, and it is a key transitional work into what I call subjective form. Pollock's subject is not coition but orgasm—and the displacement from specific sensation into the poly-referential imagery of orgasm alludes to everything that distinguishes it from Diderot's "rubbing together of membranes." The dislocations in this picture are not Cubist, but could not have been conceived without Cubism as an antecedent pattern;

169

its imagery lacks the clarity and the specifics of Surrealism. We have to reconstruct both Cubism and Surrealism in looking to realize the import of Pollock's forms. It is this necessity for our reconstruction which makes the Picassos, compared to it, illustrations, and the Matta a diagram. The theme of orgasm provides the occasion of release of feeling comparable in the painting to release from specific description and a specific plastic order, i.e. a loss of control—which is what a subjective state is. Beyond the particular subject of this painting the attitude of letting go which it embodies provides access to many kinds and instances of subjective states confronted in their full intensity.

For the letting go is the laying of the artist open to all the kinds of suggestions which he may spontaneously construe from the events on the canvas, events construed as the forms of feeling rather than things. The real role of action in Action Painting is to *reduce*, through time, the manifold of meanings which wells up even in a brief instant of entertaining the possibilities of a formal event. The action— which may include the hundreds of brush drawings which Franz Kline made on telephone-directory pages, the balletic capers and drips of Pollock, the sado-masochistic attacks of de Kooning, the painful, abortive, shuddering, laborious (and yet consummately elegant) scrapings and repaintings of Guston —all these are rehearsals and reprises of the actual movements of the mind in coming to know its own contents, in knowing what is possible for it: like a sacrament, the outward sign of an inner state. As action, it is not directed toward itself as knowing so much as toward the work as known, in the same way as desire is movement toward the desired.

Each element in the work, be it something separable like a stroke or a color, or something relational like a movement or a proportion, is, at its first appearance, a proposal for a given meaning—not wholly known, like the poet's first proposal of a word, the sense of which becomes revealed only through subsequent interlacings. The artist, in tacitly granting it a meaning, perhaps merely in beholding it as such-and-such, which may not be what another reading would take it to be, creates a context for its specification and thereby invests himself in it. The element gains not simply in plausibility, but also in tenability as it enters various relations and is recreated by them. The law of relation —which is simply that relations are elements, too— is fundamental. For not only does this describe the formality of the work—as a necessary closure of relations—but also, because the artist (and the spectator), in laying his consciousness open to the spontaneous données of seeing whatever the totality of relations can imply to him, attests to his responsibility for all the consequences that he permits. In this sense, the work is a self-discovery, but it is also a demand that the work cohere to the whole succession of terms by which it is *felt*. Actually the completion of any of the presentational forms of art in the past involved the same thing. The sculpturesque rendering of the fifteenth century both implied and assumed linear perspective; late chiaroscuro rendering implied an open spatial form, the dynamic brushstroke of Cézanne, van Gogh or Soutine was a way of making good on the dynamism of their own particular spatial-schemes; the geodesic descriptions of space and volume in Giacometti necessitate an obliteration of color. In the more representational instances in the visual arts these factors are all lumped as handwriting or style of construction whereas actually they are more fundamentally the symbols of feelings about what is represented. The completion of the form is none other than the completion of the feelings in the most accurate way. In Flaubert's phrase, the *mot juste* is also the most musical word.

In the case of abstract art, since what is constructed is not patently identifiable as separate things, the artist's motivations are sometimes regarded as purely formal accomplishments in the limited, Greenbergian sense of self-subsistent formal order, a purely physical harmony of shapes and colors. But Cubism for the Abstract-Expressionists constituted not so much a scaffolding on which to portray a purely objective order but a kind of *romance* of all the possibilities of self-representation, a field for the disclosure of internal events. Its closed-up, shallow space spoke not so much of reverence for the plane as an architectonic necessity as for the *hereness* of experience opposed to its thereness in prior pictorial art. The displacements of

Surrealism were purely illustrational, having to do with verbalizable, hence fixed, ideas. The displacements of Cubism were physical only, having to do with eye movements, visual analysis and harmonic order which was subsistent in itself.

The displacements of Abstract-Expressionism were to portray the force and interaction of the subjective forms themselves, poignantly and pointedly related, yet fleeting at the same time. It is here that the qualities of spontaneous painterliness come in. Not for the quality of the paint itself, but because of the precise adjustments in meaning and inflection that can only come out in performance rather than in planning. The dancer or the musician knows this as part of his discipline. For the painter the strain was in a sense greater because the movement was not that of body or sound but that of his own construction of the events.

We may approximate the rise of meanings in abstract form by reference to how meaning arises in representation. The only real sense in which the artists under discussion are abstract is the way the forms are author-projected, proprioceptive rather than found in the real world: they represent the unity of the subject rather than of contingency. For the represented form the artist learns at the same time an *ad hoc* solution to symbolizing a structural identity as well as a general attitudinal solution *vis-à-vis* appearance. A newly perceived quality can lead to a fresh problem which then demands a revision of language and hence a revision of the mode of experience. Impressionism, for example. At each stage of renovation there is an approval on the part of the artist of the case represented and of the kind of recognition that has taken place. At each stage, contact is made with experience and the symbolizing power of language is refreshed. In abstract art, the approval is given on more personal grounds and so the language is more hermetic—but then just to this degree the success in symbolizing must be more rigorous.

"It was Pollock," said de Kooning, "who broke the ice." The breaking of the ice was precisely this loss of control, this making themselves available to the totality of the picture. It was this, rather than any particular style, which underlay their mutual recognition and fellow-feeling during the avant-garde phase. Stylistically the characteristics diverged toward field painting on one hand and specific plasticity on the other, representing over a period of time the groupings of the Parsons and Egan galleries respectively. Pollock, Rothko, Newman, Still and Reinhardt, at Parsons, were all essentially field painters. De Kooning, Kline, Guston, Tworkov and McNeil, at Egan, are by and large painters who maintain specific plastic energies in spite of or along with the energies of the field. James Brooks and Milton Resnick have been both. The basic differences here are psychological rather than formal. They stem from how the artist entertains his meanings—whether he is engulfed by them or forces his way into them. The most powerful and suggestive paintings seem to me to be those where precisely both kinds of energy exist in a dynamic equilibrium: in Pollock's *Echo*, which has always seemed to me like an Altdorfer in its play of spatial complexity and specificity as over and against the by-now-beautiful webs; in de Kooning's *Asheville* or *Gotham News* more so than the later *Women* or *Excavation*; in Kline's *Mahoning*. The plastic, three-dimensional weightiness in these is the same that Cézanne spoke of when he said: "Nature for us men is more depth than surface."

The veracity of their method, simply because it was applied with the rigor and penetration of real need (hence the valorization of sincerity), became a method of art even despite some intentions. The demand for unity inherent in the notion of realization was unavoidable, and gave rise to structures, or more properly, to series of structures, which have irrevocably altered our sense of what can be structured at all. It is not a matter of deciding in what sense Abstract-Expressionist painting is judgeable by compositional standards so much as of testing whether any compositional proposal meets the test of felt consequentiality put forward by Abstract-Expressionism. That the work of subsequent movements has not been in this sense compositional is not surprising. By and large, later developments have not been avant-garde movements so much as exercises in rhetoric and promotion. Thus in spite

175

of many needs for art, whether as unification or as laying bare of experience, we die of thirst *auprès de la fontaine.*

If it was the nature of Abstract-Expressionism to depict what is essentially a flux, it was a necessity for it in some sense to fail. Unlike the time arts of dance, music, theater and even writing, what was essential to it was what could not actually be there. It could only be realized by a continued investment of credibility and enthusiasm which, individuals apart, we seem to experience only in the dynamic phase of a movement, before it becomes frozen into a style. Painting had to do it because the reconstruction of time in the actual time arts is too literal, too much of an illustration. Writing brings it off best, perhaps, but it cannot express real simultaneity. The avant-garde condition of Abstract-Expressionism was that its accuracy with regard to experience seemed both evident and urgent; furthermore, its standards for painting seemed complete. As the paintings themselves acquired the look of art whether the artists liked it or not, they became appealing and understandable rather than pressing and difficult. Their capacity to denote the flow of inner life became lost for most observers. The very fact of "explanation" deprives them of something.

The real fact of art in relation to the avant-garde is that it is always for the very few. The demands of our society, or indeed perhaps of any social context, run in large measure contrary to the needs of art which must be constantly reconstructed, re-enacted on an individual basis rather than in terms of some merchandising phrase. Even the premiumization of avant-gardism itself is a form of merchandising. In one sense there are only the individual works—no style, no movement. In another sense the basic assertion which did bind the works together, at least while they were being generated, persists as a critique and as a standard recoverable for the re-experiencing of all works, past and present. The abiding element will not be the particular argument which may have given them a certain currency at a certain time, but the fact that the standard was a very high one.

The Invisible
Avant-Garde

by John Ashbery

John Ashbery's article is based on a lecture he gave
at the Yale Art School in May, 1968; it was one of a
series of talks by writers and critics organized by
painter Jack Tworkov as an attempt to explore the
phenomenon of the avant-garde in present-day art.

THE fact that I, a poet, was invited by the Yale Art School to talk about the avant-garde, in one of a series of lectures under this general heading, is in itself such an eloquent characterization of the avant-garde today that no further comment seems necessary. It would appear then that this force in art which would be the very antithesis of tradition if it were to allow itself even so much of a relationship with tradition as an antithesis implies, is, on the contrary, a tradition of sorts. At any rate it can be discussed, attacked, praised, taught in seminars, just as a tradition can be. There may be a fine distinction to be made between "a" tradition and "the" tradition, but the point is that there is no

longer any doubt in anyone's mind that the vanguard *is*—it's there, before you, solid, tangible,
"alive and well," as the buttons say.

Things were very different 20 years ago when I
was a student and was beginning to experiment with
poetry. At that time it was the art and literature of
the Establishment that were traditional. There was
in fact almost no experimental poetry being written
in this country, unless you counted the rather pale
attempts of a handful of poets who were trying to
imitate some of the effects of the French Surrealists.
The situation was a little different in the other arts.
Painters like Jackson Pollock had not yet been discovered by the mass magazines—this was to come
a little later, though in fact *Life* did in 1949 print
an article on Pollock, showing some of his large drip
paintings and satirically asking whether he was the
greatest living painter in America. This was still a
long way from the decorous enthusiasm with which
Time and *Life* today greet every new kink. But the
situation was a bit better for the painters then, since
there were a lot of them doing very important work
and this fact was known to themselves and a few
critics. Poetry could boast of no such good luck.
As for music, the situation also was bleak but at
least there *was* experimental music and a few people
knew about it. It is hard to believe however that as
late as 1945 such an acceptably experimental and
posthumously successful composer as Bartok could
die in total poverty, and that until a very few years
ago such a respectable composer as Schoenberg was

considered a madman. I remember that in the spring of 1949 there was a symposium on the arts at Harvard during which a number of new works were performed including Schoenberg's *Trio for Strings*. My friend the poet Frank O'Hara who was majoring in music at Harvard went to hear it and was violently attacked for doing so by one of the young instructors in the music department, who maintained that Schoenberg was literally insane. Today the same instructor would no doubt attack him for going to hear anything so academic. To paraphrase Bernard Shaw, it is the fate of some artists, and perhaps the best ones, to pass from unacceptability to acceptance without an intervening period of appreciation.

At that time I found the avant-garde very exciting, just as the young do today, but the difference was that in 1950 there was no sure proof of the existence of the avant-garde. To experiment was to have the feeling that one was poised on some outermost brink. In other words if one wanted to depart, even moderately, from the norm, one was taking one's life—one's life as an artist—into one's hands. A painter like Pollock for instance was gambling everything on the fact that he *was* the greatest painter in America, for if he wasn't, he was nothing, and the drips would turn out to be random splashes from the brush of a careless housepainter. It must often have occurred to Pollock that there was just a possibility that he wasn't an artist at all, that he had spent his life "toiling up the wrong road to art" as Flaubert said of Zola. But this very real possibility is paradoxically just what makes the tremendous excitement in his work. It is a gamble against terrific odds. Most reckless things are beautiful in some way, and recklessness is what makes experimental art beautiful, just as religions are beautiful because of the strong possibility that they are founded on nothing. We would all believe in God if we knew He existed, but would this be much fun?

The doubt element in Pollock—and I am using him as a convenient symbol for the avant-garde artist of the previous school—is what keeps his work alive for us. Even though he has been accepted now by practically everybody from *Life* on down, or on up, his work remains unresolved. It has not congealed into masterpieces. In spite of public acceptance the doubt is there—maybe the acceptance is there because of the doubt, the vulnerability which makes it possible to love the work.

It might be argued that traditional art is even riskier than experimental art; that it can offer no very real assurances to its acolytes, and since traditions are always going out of fashion it is more dangerous and therefore more worthwhile than experimental art. This could be true, and in fact certain great artists of our time have felt it necessary to renounce the experiments of their youth just in order to save them. The poet Ron Padgett notes that the catalogue by William S. Rubin of the recent Museum of Modern Art exhibition of Dada and Surrealism praises Picabia's early work but ruefully assumes that with his later work he had "passed

Paul Signac: *Le Dimanche Parisien*, 1889. Marlborough Gallery.

Gino Severini: *Self-Portrait with Boater,* ca. 1912, black chalk, 21½ inches high. Art Institute of Chicago.

Gino Severini: *Dancer*, ca. 1915, 39⅜ inches high.
Guggenheim Museum, New York.

Etienne Boullée's truncated tower design, 1780.

Hermann Obrist's monument project, 1902.

ПРОЛЕТАРИИ

42

ATELIER LISSITZKY
1920

El Lissitzky's 1920 design for a Lenin Tribune project.

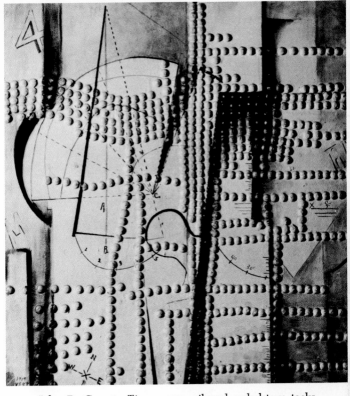

John R. Covert: *Time*, 1919, oil and upholstery tacks, 25⅝ inches high. Yale University Art Gallery, New Haven.

Katherine S. Dreier: *Abstract Portrait of Marcel Duchamp*, 1918, 18 inches high. Museum of Modern Art, New York.

out of serious consideration as a painter." Padgett goes on to say, "A parallel example is provided by de Chirico, whom many feel betrayed his own best interests as a painter. Possibly so. But in Picabia's case, the curiosity that compelled him to go on to become a less 'attractive' painter is the same that carried his adventure into Dada in the first place, and it is this spirit, as much as the paintings themselves, which is significant." I think one could expand this argument to cover de Chirico and Duchamp as well. The former passed from being one of the greatest painters of this century to a crotchety fabricator of bad pictures who refuses to hear any good said of his early period, but he did so with such a vengeance that his act almost becomes exemplary. And Duchamp's silence *is* exemplary without question for a whole generation of young artists.

Therefore it is a question of distinguishing bad traditional art and bad avant-garde art from good traditional art and good avant-garde art. But after one has done this one still has a problem with good traditional art. One can assume that good avant-garde art will go on living because the mere fact of its having been able to struggle into life at all will keep it alive. The doubt remains. But good traditional art may disappear at any moment when the tradition founders. It is a perilous business. I would class de Chirico's late paintings as good traditional art, though as bad art, because they embrace a tradition which everything in the artist's career seemed to point away from, and which he therefore accepted because, no doubt, he felt as an avant-garde artist that only the unacceptable is acceptable. On the other hand a painter like Thomas Hart Benton, who was Pollock's teacher, was at his best a better painter than de Chirico is now, but is a worse artist because he accepted the acceptable. *Life* used to have an article on Benton almost every month, showing his murals for some new post office or library. The fact that *Life* switched its affections from Benton to Pollock does not make either of them any worse, but it does illustrate that Benton's is the kind of art that cannot go on living without acceptance, while Pollock's is of the kind which cannot be destroyed by acceptance, since it is basically unacceptable.

What has happened since Pollock? The usual explanation is that "media" have multiplied to such an extent that it is no longer possible for secrets to remain secret very long, and that this has had the effect of turning the avant-garde from a small contingent of foolhardy warriors into a vast and well equipped regiment. In fact the avant-garde has absorbed most of the army, or vice versa—in any case the result is that the avant-garde can now barely exist because of the immense amounts of attention and money that are focused on it, and that the only artists who have any privacy are the handful of decrepit stragglers behind the big booming avant-garde juggernaut. This does seem to be what has happened. I was amazed the other night while watching the news on television when the announcer took up a new book by the young experimental poet Aram Saroyan and read it aloud to the audience from beginning to end. It is true that this took only a couple of minutes and that it was done for purposes of a putdown—nevertheless we know that the way of the mass mediums is to pass from putdown to panegyric without going through a transitional phase of straight reportage, and it may be only a matter of weeks before Aram Saroyan has joined Andy Warhol and Viva and the rest of the avant-garde on the "Tonight" show.

Looking back only as far as the beginning of this century we see that the period of neglect for an avant-garde artist has shrunk for each generation. Picasso was painting mature masterpieces for at least ten years before he became known even to a handful of collectors. Pollock's incubation period was a little shorter. But since then the period has grown shorter each year so that it now seems to be something like a minute. It is no longer possible, or it seems no longer possible, for an important avant-garde artist to go unrecognized. And, sadly enough, his creative life-expectancy has dwindled correspondingly, since artists are no fun once they have been discovered. Gertrude Stein wrote in *The Autobiography of Alice B. Toklas*: "She says she likes what she has and she likes the adventure of a new one. That is what she always says about young painters, about anything, once everybody knows they are good the adventure is over. And, adds

Picasso with a sigh, even after everybody knows they are good, not any more people really like them than they did when only the few knew they were good." And Dylan Thomas summed it up when he wrote that he had once been happy and unknown and that he was now miserable and acclaimed.

I am not convinced that it is "media" that are responsible for all this—there have always been mediums of one sort or another and they have taken up the cause of the avant-garde only recently. I am at a loss to say what it is, unless that it is that events during the first decades of this century eventually ended up proving that the avant-garde artist is a kind of hero, and that a hero is, of course, what everybody wants to be. We all have to be first, and it is now certain—as it was not, I think, before—that the experimenting artist does something first, even though it may be discarded later on. So that, paradoxically, it is safest to experiment. Only a few artists like de Chirico have realized the fallacy of this argument, and since his course was to reject his own genius and produce inferior art it is unlikely that many artists will follow him.

What then must the avant-garde artist do to remain avant-garde? For it has by now become a question of survival both of the artist and of the individual. In both art and life today we are in danger of substituting one conformity for another, or, to use a French expression, of trading one's one-eyed horse for a blind one. Protests against the mediocre values of our society such as the Hippie movement seem to imply that one's only way out is to join a parallel society whose stereotyped manners, language, speech and dress are only reverse images of the one it is trying to reject. We feel in America that we have to join something, that our lives are directionless unless we are part of a group, a clan— an idea very different from the European one, where even friendships are considered not very important and life centers around oneself and one's partner, an extension of oneself. Is there nothing then between the extremes of Levittown and Haight-Ashbury, between an avant-garde which has become a tradition and a tradition which is no longer one? In other words, has tradition finally managed to absorb the individual talent?

On the other hand, perhaps these are the most exciting times for young artists, who must fight even harder to preserve their identity. Before they were fighting against general neglect, even hostility, but this seemed like a natural thing and therefore the fight could be carried on in good faith. Today one must fight acceptance which is much harder because it seems that one is fighting oneself.

If people like what I do, am I to assume that what I do is bad, since public opinion has always begun by rejecting what is original and new?

Perhaps the answer is not to reject what one has done, nor to be forced into a retrograde position, but merely to take into account that if one's work automatically finds acceptance, there may be a possibility that it could be improved. The Midas-like position into which our present acceptance-world forces the avant-garde is actually a disguised blessing which previous artists have not been able to enjoy, because it points the way out of the predicament it sets up—that is, toward an attitude which neither accepts nor rejects acceptance but is independent of it. Previously, vanguard artists never had to face the problems of integration into the art of their time because this usually happened at the end of a long career when the direction their art would take had long been fixed. When it took place earlier it could be dealt with in an explosion of bad temper, like Schoenberg's possibly apocryphal one when someone finally learned to play his violin concerto and he stormed out of the concert hall, vowing to write another one that *nobody* would be able to play.

Today the avant-garde has come full circle—the artist who wants to experiment is again faced with what seems like a dead end, except that instead of creating in a vacuum he is now at the center of a cheering mob. Neither climate is exactly ideal for discovery, yet both are conducive to it because they force him to take steps that he hadn't planned on. And today's young artist has the additional advantage of a fuller awareness of the hazards that lie in wait for him. He must now bear in mind that *he*, not *it*, is the avant-garde.

A few remarks by Busoni in his book *The Essence of Music* seem to apply to all the arts and also to the situation of the experimental artist today. Busoni's music has the unique quality of being excellent and of sounding like nobody else's; it has not even been successfully imitated. The essays that make up the book were written about the time of World War I when a crisis had developed in German music, involving on the one hand Expressionists like Schoenberg, of whom he disapproved, and of pedantic neo-classicists like Reger of whom he equally disapproved—a crisis which, without going into details, rather parallels that in the arts today. Somehow Busoni alone managed to avoid these extremes by taking what was valid in each and forging a totality.

He wrote: "I am a worshipper of Form—I have remained sufficiently a Latin for that. But I demand —no! the organism of art demands—that every idea fashion its own form for itself; the organism—not I —revolts against having one single form for all ideas; today especially and how much more in the coming centuries.

"The creator really only strives for perfection. And as he brings this into harmony with his individuality a new law arises unintentionally.

"The 'new' is included in the idea of 'Creation'— for in that way creation is distinguished from imitation.

"One follows a great example most faithfully if one does not follow it, for it was through turning away from its predecessor that the example became great."

And finally, in an article addressed to his pupils he wrote, "Build up! But do not content yourself any longer with self-complacent experiments and the glory of the success of the season; but turn towards the perfection of the work seriously and joyfully. Only he who looks toward the future looks cheerfully."

What Is Pop Art?

Interviews by G. R. Swenson

with Roy Lichtenstein. Andy Warhol and Jasper Johns

The late G. R. Swenson was one of the
first critics to take Pop Art seriously.

Roy Lichtenstein

What is Pop Art?

I don't know—the use of commercial art as subject matter in painting, I suppose. It was hard to get
a painting that was despicable enough so that no
one would hang it—everybody was hanging everything. It was almost acceptable to hang a dripping
paint rag, everybody was accustomed to this. The
one thing everyone hated was commercial art; apparently they didn't hate that enough either.

Is Pop Art despicable?

That doesn't sound so good, does it? Well, it *is*
an involvement with what I think to be the most

brazen and threatening characteristics of our culture, things we hate, but which are also powerful in their impingement on us. I think art since Cézanne has become extremely romantic and unrealistic, feeding on art: it is utopian. It has had less and less to do with the world, it looks inward—neo-Zen and all that. This is not so much a criticism as an obvious observation. Outside is the world; it's there. Pop Art looks out into the world; it appears to accept its environment, which is not good or bad, but different —another state of mind.

How can you like exploitation? How can you like the complete mechanization of work? How can you like bad art? I have to answer that I accept it as being there, in the world.

Are you anti-experimental?

I think so, and anti-contemplative, anti-nuance, anti-getting-away-from-the-tyranny-of-the-rectangle, anti-movement-and-light, anti-mystery, anti-paint-quality, anti-Zen, and anti all of those brilliant ideas of preceding movements which everyone under-stands so thoroughly.

We like to think of industrialization as being despicable. I don't really know what to make of it. There's something terribly brittle about it. I suppose I would still prefer to sit under a tree with a picnic basket rather than under a gas pump, but signs and comic strips are interesting as subject matter. There are certain things that are usable, forceful and vital

about commercial art. We're using those things—
but we're not really advocating stupidity, international teenagerism and terrorism.

Where did your ideas about art begin?

The ideas of Prof. Hoyt Sherman [at Ohio State
University] on perception were my earliest important influence and still affect my ideas of visual
unity.

Perception?

Yes. Organized perception is what art is all about.

He taught you "how to look?"

Yes. He taught me how to go about learning how
to look.

At what?

At what, doesn't have anything to do with it. It
is a process. It has nothing to do with any external
form the painting takes, it has to do with a way of
building a unified pattern of seeing. . . . In Abstract-
Expressionism the paintings symbolize the idea of
ground-directedness as opposed to object-directed-
ness. You put something down, react to it, put something else down, and the painting itself becomes a
symbol of this. The difference is that rather than
symbolize this ground-directedness I do an object-
directed appearing thing. There is humor here. The

work is still ground-directed; the fact that it's an eyebrow or an almost direct copy of something is unimportant. The ground-directedness is in the painter's mind and not immediately apparent in the painting. Pop Art makes the statement that ground-directedness is not a quality that the painting has because of what it looks like. . . . This tension between apparent object-directed products and actual ground-directed processes is an important strength of Pop Art.

Antagonistic critics say that Pop Art does not transform its models. Does it?

Transformation is a strange word to use. It implies that art transforms. It doesn't, it just plain forms. Artists have never worked with the model—just with the painting. What you're really saying is that an artist like Cézanne transforms what we think the painting ought to look like into something he thinks it ought to look like. He's working with paint, not nature; he's making a painting, he's forming. I think my work is different from comic strips—but I wouldn't call it transformation; I don't think that whatever is meant by it is important to art. What I do is form, whereas the comic strip is not formed in the sense I'm using the word; the comics have shapes but there has been no effort to make them intensely unified. The purpose is different, one intends to depict and I intend to unify. And my work is actually different from comic strips in that every mark is really in a different place, however slight the difference seems to some. The difference is often not great, but it is crucial. People also consider my work to be anti-art in the same way they consider it pure depiction, "not transformed." I don't feel it is anti-art.

There is no neat way of telling whether a work of art is composed or not; we're too comfortable with ideas that art is the battleground for interaction, that with more and more experience you become more able to compose. It's true, everybody accepts that; it's just that the idea no longer has any power.

Abstract-Expressionism has had an almost universal influence on the arts. Will Pop Art?

I don't know. I doubt it. It seems too particular— too much the expression of a few personalities. Pop might be a difficult starting point for a painter. He would have great difficulty in making these brittle images yield to compositional purposes. . . . Interaction between painter and painting is not the total commitment of Pop, but it is still a major concern —though concealed and strained.

Do you think that an idea in painting—whether it be 'interaction' or the use of commercial art—gets progressively less powerful with time?

It seems to work that way. Cubist and Action Painting ideas, although originally formidable and still an influence, are less crucial to us now. Some individual artists, though—Stuart Davis, for example —seem to get better and better.

A curator at the Modern Museum has called Pop Art fascistic and militaristic.

The heroes depicted in comic books are fascist types, but I don't take them seriously in these paintings—maybe there is a point in not taking them seriously, a political point. I use them for purely formal reasons, and that's not what those heroes were invented for. . . . Pop Art has very immediate and of-the-moment meanings which will vanish— that kind of thing is ephemeral—and Pop takes advantage of this "meaning," which is not supposed to last, to divert you from its formal content. I think the formal statement in my work will become clearer in time. Superficially, Pop seems to be all subject matter, whereas Abstract-Expressionism, for example, seems to be all esthetic. . . .

I paint directly—then it's said to be an exact copy, and not art, probably because there's no perspective or shading. It doesn't look like a painting *of* something, it looks like the thing itself. Instead of looking like a painting *of* a billboard—the way a Reginald Marsh would look—Pop Art seems to be the actual thing. It is an intensification, a stylistic intensification of the excitement which the subject matter has for me; but the style is, as you said, cool. One of the things a cartoon does is to express violent emotion and passion in a completely mechanical and removed style. To express this thing in a painterly style would dilute it; the techniques I use are not commercial, they only appear to be commercial—and the ways of seeing and composing and unifying are different and have different ends.

Is Pop Art American?

Everybody has called Pop Art "American" painting, but it's actually industrial painting. America was hit by industrialism and capitalism harder and sooner and its values seem more askew. . . . I think the meaning of my work is that it's industrial, it's what all the world will soon become. Europe will be the same way, soon, so it won't be American; it will be universal.

Andy Warhol

Someone said that Brecht wanted everyone to think alike. I want everyone to think alike. But Brecht wanted to do it through Communism, in a way. Russia is doing it under government. It's happening here all by itself without being under a strict government; so if it's working without trying, why can't it work without being Communist? Everybody looks alike and acts alike, and we're getting more and more that way.

I think everybody should be a machine.

I think everybody should like everybody.

Is that what Pop Art is all about?

Yes. It's liking things.

And liking things is like being a machine?

Yes, because you do the same thing every time. You do it over and over again.

And you approve of that?

Yes, because it's all fantasy. It's hard to be creative and it's also hard not to think what you do is creative or hard not to be called creative because everybody is always talking about that and individuality. Everybody's always being creative. And it's so funny when you say things aren't, like the shoe I would draw for an advertisement was called a "creation" but the drawing of it was not. But I guess I believe in both ways. All these people who aren't very good should be really good. Everybody is too good now, really. Like, how many actors are there? There are millions of actors. They're all pretty good. And how many painters are there? Millions of painters and all pretty good. How can you say one style is better than another? You ought to be able to be an Abstract-Expressionist next week, or a Pop artist, or a realist, without feeling you've given up something. I think the artists who aren't very good should become like everybody else so that people would like things that aren't very good.

It's already happening. All you have to do is read the magazines and the catalogues. It's this style or that style, this or that image of man—but that really doesn't make any difference. Some artists get left out that way, and why should they?

Is Pop Art a fad?

Yes, it's a fad, but I don't see what difference it makes. I just heard a rumor that G. quit working, that she's given up art altogether. And everyone is saying how awful it is that A. gave up his style and is doing it in a different way. I don't think so at all. If an artist can't do any more, then he should just quit; and an artist ought to be able to change his style without feeling bad. I heard that Lichtenstein said he might not be painting comic strips a year or two from now—I think that would be so great, to be able to change styles. And I think that's what's going to happen, that's going to be the whole new scene. That's probably one reason I'm using silk screens now. I think somebody should be able to do all my paintings for me. I haven't been able to make every image clear and simple and the same as the first one. I think it would be so great if more people took up silk screens so that no one would know whether my picture was mine or somebody else's.

It would turn art history upside down?

Yes.

Is that your aim?

No. The reason I'm painting this way is that I want to be a machine, and I feel that whatever I do and do machine-like is what I want to do.

Was commercial art more machine-like?

No, it wasn't. I was getting paid for it, and did anything they told me to do. If they told me to draw a shoe, I'd do it, and if they told me to correct it, I would—I'd do anything they told me to do, correct it and do it right. I'd have to invent and now I don't; after all that "correction," those commercial drawings would have feelings, they would have a style. The attitude of those who hired me had feeling or something to it; they knew what they wanted, they insisted; sometimes they got very emotional. The process of doing work in commercial art was machine-like, but the attitude had feeling to it.

Why did you start painting soup cans?

Because I used to drink it. I used to have the same lunch every day, for twenty years, I guess, the same thing over and over again. Someone said my life has dominated me; I liked that idea. I used to want to live at the Waldorf Towers and have soup and a sandwich, like that scene in the restaurant in *Naked Lunch.* . . .

We went to see *Dr. No* at Forty-second Street. It's a fantastic movie, so cool. We walked outside and somebody threw a cherry bomb right in front of us, in this big crowd. And there was blood, I saw blood on people and all over. I felt like I was bleeding all over. I saw in the paper last week that there are more people throwing them—it's just part of the scene—and hurting people. My show in Paris is going to be called "Death in America." I'll show the electric-chair pictures and the dogs in Birmingham and car wrecks and some suicide pictures.

Why did you start these "Death" pictures?

I believe in it. Did you see the *Enquirer* this week? It had "The Wreck that Made Cops Cry"— a head cut in half, the arms and hands just lying there. It's sick, but I'm sure it happens all the time. I've met a lot of cops recently. They take pictures of everything, only it's almost impossible to get pictures from them.

When did you start with the "Death" series?

I guess it was the big plane crash picture, the front page of a newspaper: 129 DIE. I was also painting the "Marilyns." I realized that everything I was doing must have been Death. It was Christmas or Labor Day—a holiday—and every time you turned on the radio they said something like, "4 million are going to die." That started it. But when you see a gruesome picture over and over again, it doesn't really have any effect.

But you're still doing "Elizabeth Taylor" pictures.

I started those a long time ago, when she was so sick and everybody said she was going to die. Now I'm doing them all over, putting bright colors on her lips and eyes.

My next series will be pornographic pictures. They will look blank; when you turn on the black lights, then you see them—big breasts and. . . . If a cop came in, you could just flick out the lights or turn on the regular lights—how could you say that was pornography? But I'm still just practicing with these yet. Segal did a sculpture of two people making love, but he cut it all up, I guess because he thought it was too pornographic to be art. Actually it was very beautiful, perhaps a little too good, or he may feel a little protective about art. When you read Genêt you get all hot, and that makes some people say this is not art. The thing I like about it is that it makes you forget about style and that sort of thing; style isn't really important.

Is "Pop" a bad name?

The name sounds so awful. Dada must have something to do with Pop—it's so funny, the names are really synonyms. Does anyone know what they're supposed to mean or have to do with, those names? Johns and Rauschenberg—Neo-Dada for all these years, and everyone calling them derivative and unable to transform the things they use—are now called progenitors of Pop. It's funny the way things change. I think John Cage has been very influential, and Merce Cunningham, too, maybe. Did you see that article in the *Hudson Review* ["The End of the Renaissance?" Summer, 1963]? It was about Cage and that whole crowd, but with a lot of big words like radical empiricism and teleology. Who knows? Maybe Jap and Bob were Neo-Dada and aren't any more. History books are being rewritten all the time. It doesn't matter what you do. Everybody just goes on thinking the same thing, and every year it gets more and more alike. Those who talk about individuality the most are the ones who most object to deviation, and in a few years it may be the other way around. Some day everybody will think just what they want to think, and then everybody will probably be thinking alike; that seems to be what is happening.

Jasper Johns

What is Pop Art?

There has been an attempt to say that those classified under that term use images from the popular representations of things. Isn't that so?

Possibly. But people like Dine and Indiana—even you were included in the exhibitions . . .

I'm not a Pop artist! Once a term is set, everybody tries to relate anybody they can to it because there are so few terms in the art world. Labeling is a popular way of dealing with things.

Is there any term you object to?

I object to none any more. I used to object to each as it occurred.

It has been said that the new attitude toward painting is "cool." Is yours?

Cool or hot, one way seems just about as good as another. Whatever you're thinking or feeling, you're left with what you do; the painting is what you've done. Some painters, perhaps, rely on particular emotions. They attempt to establish certain emotional situations for themselves and that's the way they like to work.

I've taken different attitudes at different times. That allows different kinds of actions. In focusing your eye or your mind, if you focus in one way, your actions will tend to be of one nature; if you focus another way, they will be different. I prefer work that appears to come out of a changing focus—not just one relationship or even a number of them but constantly changing and shifting relationships to things in terms of focus. Often, however, one is very single-minded and pursues one particular point; often one is blind to the fact that there is another way to see what is there.

Are you aspiring to objectivity?

My paintings are not simply expressive gestures. Some of them I have thought of as facts, or at any rate there has been some attempt to say that a thing has a certain nature. Saying that, one hopes to avoid saying I feel this way about this thing; one says this thing is this thing, and one responds to what one thinks is so.

I am concerned with a thing's not being what it was, with its becoming something other than what it is, with any moment in which one identifies a thing precisely and with the slipping away of that moment, with at any moment seeing or saying and letting it go at that.

What would you consider the difference between subject matter and content, between what is depicted and what it means?

Meaning implies that something is happening; you can say meaning is determined by the use of the thing, the way an audience uses a painting once it is put in public. When you speak of what is depicted, I tend to think in terms of an intention. But the intention is usually with the artist. "Subject matter"? Where would you focus to determine subject matter?

What a thing is. In your "Device" paintings it would be the ruler.

Why do you pick ruler rather than wood or varnish or any other element? What it is—subject matter, then—is simply determined by what you're willing to say it is. What it means is simply a question of what you're willing to let it do.

There is a great deal of intention in painting; it's rather unavoidable. But when a work is let out by the artist and said to be complete, the intention loosens. Then it's subject to all kinds of use and misuse and pun. Occasionally someone will see the work in a way that even changes its significance for the person who made it; the work is no longer "intention," but the thing being seen and someone responding to it. They will see it in a way that makes you think, that is a possible way of seeing it. Then you, as the artist, can enjoy it—that's possible—or you can lament it. If you like, you can try to express the intention more clearly in another work. But what is interesting is anyone having the experiences he has.

Are you talking about the viewer or the artist?

I think either. We're not ants or bees; I don't see that we ought to take limited roles in relationship to things. I think one might just as well pretend that he is the center of what he's doing and what his experience is, and that it's only he who can do it.

If you cast a beer can, is that a comment?

On what?

On beer cans or society. When you deal with things in the world, social attitudes are connected with them—aren't they?

Basically, artists work out of rather stupid kinds of impulses and then the work is done. After that the work is used. In terms of comment, the work probably has it, some aspect which resembles language. Publicly a work becomes not just intention, but the way it is used. If an artist makes something—or if you make chewing gum and everybody ends up using it as glue, whoever made it is given the responsibility of making glue, even if what he really intends is chewing gum. You can't control that kind of thing. As far as beginning to make a work, one can do it for any reason.

If you cast a beer can, you don't have to have a social attitude to beer cans or art?

No. It occurs to me you're talking about *my* beer cans, which have a story behind them. I was doing at that time sculptures of small objects—flashlights and light bulbs. Then I heard a story about Willem de Kooning. He was annoyed with my dealer, Leo Castelli, for some reason, and said something like, "That son-of-a-bitch; you could give him two beer cans and he could sell them." I heard this and thought, "What a sculpture—two beer cans." It seemed to me to fit in perfectly with what I was doing, so I did them—and Leo sold them.

Should an artist accept suggestions—or his environment—so easily?

I think basically that's a false way of thinking. Accept or reject, where's the ease or the difficulty? I don't put any value on a kind of thinking that puts limits on things. I prefer that the artist does what he does than that, after he's done it, someone says he shouldn't have done it. I would encourage everybody to do more rather than less. I think one has to assume that the artist is free to do what he pleases so that whatever he does is his own business, that he had choices, that he could do something else.

But shouldn't the artist have an attitude to his subject, shouldn't he transform it?

Transformation is in the head. If you have one thing and make another thing, there is no transformation, but there are two things. I don't think you would mistake one for another.

Does art change with time?

One can be content just to do something over and over again in a kind of blindness. But every aspect of a work of art changes in time, in five minutes or longer.

Some painters have tried to paint Ageless Art.

The whole business here in America, of my train-ing and even more the people before me, was rooted in the mythology that the artist was separated and isolated from society and working alone, unap-preciated, then dying and after that his work be-coming very valuable, and that this was sad. That was part of the way I was trained. I think it's even less true than thinking that one is finding one's own values in the act of painting. One does it—paints—and wishes to do it. If not, you're making it into a kind of martyr situation which doesn't interest me very much.

With what has been called the "New Audience" that situation seems reversed.

Things are picked up and publicized as quickly as the mediums for doing those things allow. To say it is bad one has to have some idea about the social role art *should* have, that communication about art should be restricted because artists have a secret weapon or something which shouldn't be announced for twenty years for some reason—or because it may go out of date or someone will find something better. It's silly to say that art shouldn't get to be so well known so quickly. How quickly should it get to be known? It should be publicized just as quickly as somebody wants to publicize it.

But weren't you just saying that art should not be used as a social force?

For myself I would choose to be as much as possible outside that area. It's difficult because we are constantly faced with social situations and our work is being used in ways we didn't ask for it to be used. We see it being done. We're not idiots.

Then is it being misused in a social situation?

My point of view tends to be that work is being misused in *most* situations. Nevertheless I find it a very interesting possibility, that one can't control the situation, the way one's work is viewed, that once one offers it to be seen then anybody is able to see it as he pleases.

Pinpointing Happenings

by Allan Kaprow

Allan Kaprow, founder and chief protagonist of Happenings, is also the author of the definitive book on the subject: *Assemblage, Environments and Happenings.*

Charles Sheeler: *Self-Portrait*, 1923, crayon, watercolor, and pencil, 19¾ inches high. Museum of Modern Art, New York.

Gerald Murphy: *Watch,* 1923, 6 feet high. Dallas Museum of Fine Arts.

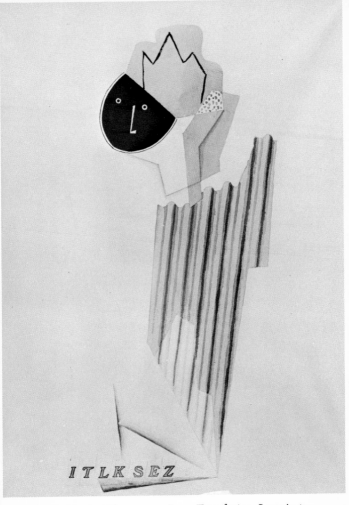

Stuart Davis: *Itlksez*, 1921. Lane Foundation, Leominster, Mass.

Man Ray: *The Enigma of Isidore Ducasse*, 1920 (replica, 1967), cloth and rope over sewing machine, 16 inches high. Museum of Modern Art, New York.

Robert Motherwell: *Elegy to the Spanish Republic, LVII,* 1957-60, 84¼ inches high. Collection of Mr. and Mrs. Gardiner Hempel, Littleton, Colorado.

Willem de Kooning: *Study for Backdrop*, 1946, 22 inches high. Private collection, New York.

Jackson Pollack: *Echo,* 1951, 92 inches high. Collection of Mr. and Mrs. Ben Heller, New York.

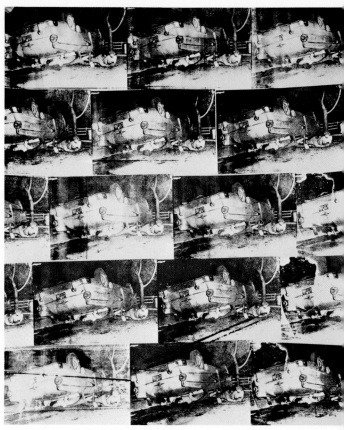

Andy Warhol: *Black and White Disaster, 4,* 1963, 82 inches high. Private collection, New York.

FROM now on, anyone who would write or speak intelligently about Happenings must declare what sort of phenomenon he is referring to; "Happening" is a household word. Yet it means almost anything to the households which hear it and use it. Consider the following:

A few seasons ago, an issue of *The New Republic* with a lead article on the political campaign of Bobby Kennedy, headlined on the cover "Bobby Kennedy Is a Happening."

Howard Moody, minister of New York's Judson Church, sent me a reprint of an excellent sermon called "Christmas Is a Happening."

Disc-jockey Murray the K formerly punctuated

his hyped-up delivery with "It's what's *happening*, baby!" In his new job with station WOR-FM, his now-modulated voice carefully grooms the call-letters as "The Happening Station."

A cosmetics commercial, composed of a swirl of gimmicked, suggestive noises leading to the name of the product, ends sexily "That was a Happening —by Revlon."

Manhattan's former Parks Commissioner, inaugurating The Great Year of the Spiritual Thaw, sponsored paint-ins, reserved the park for cyclists on Sundays, flew kites in Sheep Meadow, had a water-splash on the lake, demonstrated some fancy ice skating, officialized snowball throwing, invited the public to a star-gazing, and throughout gave the city a phrase to explain it all: "Hoving's Happenings."

Hippie groups, discotheques, PTA meetings, Rotary Club outings, a popular rock 'n' roll band, a hit record by The Supremes, a party game kit, at least two regular-run movies—are all called Happenings.

The Saturday Review asked recently in a feature article if American history was not a Happening; there was even a news analyst last winter who cynically judged our war in Vietnam as "a Happening gone out of control."

But everything came together one Sunday in January. In *The New York Times* magazine, a piece on furniture design was titled "1966 Was a Happening." It summed up an entire year of our lives. The clear implication was that *life itself* is a Happening. And in a special sense perhaps it is, although what this sense is will have to come later.

What do the 50 or so Happeners around the world think a Happening is? With them, too, the variety of opinion is disconcerting. Most, including myself, have tried to get rid of the word "Happening," but this seems futile by now. Hence, granting a certain amount of oversimplification, there appear to be roughly six directions prevalent. Among them there is a fair amount of overlapping and continuous recombination. However, as difficult as it may be to find a pure Happening of each sort, the future critic will find it useful to identify as nearly as possible the kind of work he is talking about. (There is as much difference between some Happenings as there is between Beethoven and Hershey's chocolate bars.)

First there is the *Night Club* or *Cock Fight* or *Pocket Drama* style, in which small audiences meet in cellars, rooms or studios. They press close around the performers and are occasionally drawn into the action in some simple way. Jazz may be played, a couple may make love, food may be cooked, a film may be projected, furniture may be battered to bits, paper torn into shreds, dance-like movements may occur, lights may change colors, poetry or words of all kinds may pour forth from loudspeakers, perhaps superimposed or in unusual order. Throughout, a mood of intense intimacy will prevail.

219

An extension of this type of Happening is the *Extravaganza*. Presented on stages and in arenas to large audiences, it takes the form of a fairly lavish compendium of the modern arts—with dancers, actors, poets, painters, musicians, etc., all contributing talents. In basic concept (probably unconsciously) the Extravaganza is an updated Wagnerian opera, a *Gesamtkunstwerk*. Its character and methods, however, are usually (though not always) more lighthearted, resembling three-ring circuses and vaudeville reviews in the way that these were developed by Dada and Surrealist antecedents. This Happening is the only kind with which the public has any familiarity and, incidentally, with which it feels some degree of comfort. Watered-down, it has emerged as the stock-in-trade of the discotheque and psychedelic scene.

Then there is the *Event*, in which an audience, again usually seated in a theater, watches a brief occurrence such as a single light going on and off, or a trumpet sounding while a balloon emerges from its bell until it bursts. Or, there is a prolongation of a unitary action such as a man walking back and forth across the stage for two hours. Most frequently, dead-pan wit joins, or alternates with, disciplined attentiveness to small or normally unimportant phenomena.

Next is the *Guided Tour* or *Pied Piper* kind of Happening. A selected group of people is led through the countryside or around a city, through buildings, backyards, parks and shops. They observe things, are given instructions, are lectured to, discover things happening to them—all of both an ordinary and extraordinary sort. In this mode, the intended focus upon a mixture of the commonplace and fantastic makes the journey a modern equivalent to Dante's spiritual one. The creator of this Happening is more than a cicerone; he is in effect a Virgil with a message.

The fifth is almost entirely mental. It is *Idea* art or literary *Suggestion* when it is written down in its usual form of short notes. "It's raining in Tokyo"; "Fill a glass of water for two days"; "Over there"; "Red light on the Brooklyn Bridge," are examples. They may be enacted, but need not be (and often are not). Following the Duchampian implication that art is what is in the mind of the beholder, who can make art or non-art at will, a thought is as valuable as an action. The mere notion that the world is full of "ready-made" activities permits one quite seriously to "sign" the whole earth or any part of it, without actually doing a thing. The responsibility for such quasi-art is thus thrown entirely upon the shoulders of any individual who cares to accept it. The rest is primarily contemplative, but may lead in time to meaningful action.

The sixth and last kind of Happening is the *Activity* type. It is directly involved in the everyday world, ignores theaters and audiences, is more active than meditative, and is close in spirit to physical sports, ceremonies, fairs, mountain climbing, war games and political demonstrations. It also partakes of the unconscious daily rituals of the supermarkets, subway rides at rush-hours and toothbrushing every morning. The Activity Happening selects and combines situations to be participated-in, rather than watched or just thought-about.

Of the six categories of Happenings, the last appears to me most compelling, if indeed most risky. It is the least encumbered by artistic precedents, is the least professionalistic and is free, therefore, to confront the question raised earlier, of whether life is a Happening or a Happening is an art of life. This seems preferable to defending the Happening from the very start *as* an art form. The Activity type, of course, is risky because it easily loses the clarity of its paradoxical position of being art-life or life-art. Habit may lead the Happener to depend on certain favored situations and to perfect them in the manner of the conventional artist. Or his choices may become so indistinguishable from daily events that participation degenerates into routine and indifference. Either way, he will have lost the handshake between himself, his co-participants and the environment.

It is possible now to consider the difference between this and an advertising campaign, a commuter train ride, the stock exchange. Or, if these seem too prosaic—notwithstanding the fact that some Happenings are deliberately prosaic—there is the recent Alaska earthquake, the Candy Mossler murder trial, the Buddhist monk who burned himself in Saigon and, for piquant relief, the Mad Litterbug who periodically covers several city blocks in New York with paper cut-outs.

Clearly it can be assumed that none of these examples was initially a Happening. Yet any of them *could* be if some Happener wished to include them in his way of working. The distinction is simply that of assigning a new or multiple set of functions to a situation normally bound by convention; at the very least, it is *consciousness of this possibility.* Candy Mossler was a female impersonator whose every appearance in the newspapers caused those in the Happening to dress as she did and privately tape-record their thoughts. These were later sent to Mrs. Mossler signed with her name and address.

A Happening is always a purposive activity, whether it is game-like, ritualistic or purely contemplative. (It may even have as its purpose no purpose.) Having a purpose may be a way of paying attention to what is commonly not noticed. Purpose implies a selective operation for every Happening, limiting it to only certain situations out of countless options. The selections made by individual Happeners are as personal as their influences upon lesser figures are obvious. The expressive character of the selection of image-situations may be assertive or passive, but the *fact* of the choice suggests value: what is presented is worthwhile in some way. What is left out by virtue of its very exclusion is less worthwhile for the time being: it is withheld from our attention. If life can be a Happening, it is only a small portion of life that can be apprehended that way; and only a Happener will make the decision to so apprehend it. If we were speaking of painting or music, all this would seem truistic. But in view of the vast and giddy nonsense about what Happenings are, it seemed necessary to point to some of their actual characteristics.

Like much social endeavor, and like all creative endeavor, Happenings are moral activity, if only by implication. Moral intelligence, in contrast to moralism or sermonizing, is what comes alive in a field of pressing alternatives. Moral certainty tends at best to be pious, sentimental; at worst pietistic. The Happenings in their various modes, resemble the best efforts of contemporary inquiry into identity and meaning, for they take their stand in the midst of the modern information deluge. In such a plethora of possible choices, they may be among the most responsible acts of our time.

The Experience of Kinesis

by Michael Kirby

Michael Kirby is the author of a book on Happenings, has produced Happenings himself, and has shown his sculpture-constructions at Finch College.

To discuss kinetic sculpture in socio-political terms and relate it to the media-dominated, automated, mechanized, scientific character of our historical moment may, in some cases, be quite interesting, but it tells us nothing about the work as art. By ignoring and blurring the distinctions between individual works, it creates the kind of generic over-simplification that, in the cases of Pop and Op, brought discomfort to many artists and satisfaction only to the dilettante. Kinetic sculpture—in using the term I refer to all works which involve motion, whether the motion of light, 3-dimensional elements, or whatever—is being produced in impressive and constantly increasing diversity, and it is much more important to analyze and elucidate that diversity than it is to explain away important differences in order to create a new "ism."

The complete description of sculpture that involves motion involves many parameters, but perhaps the most important is that of time. Movement is obviously dependent upon time, and the experience of time would seem to be at the heart of any esthetics of kinetic sculpture. If, in a very basic and fundamental way, the structure of painting is two-dimensional and the structure of sculpture is three-dimensional, the structure of kinetic sculpture is four-dimensional: it is the structuring of time. But experience of, and in, time can have a wide diversity. We can say that there are four distinct modes in the experience of kinesis. "Pure" examples of each mode exist. And the fact that they can, at times, overlap and blend one into the other does not deny their theoretical implications.

The most complicated of the four modes involves memory and expectancy and their relationship. It is possible that each moment in the perception of a work changing with time—whether it is music, drama, dance, or kinetic sculpture—becomes charged with expectations about the future nature of the work. Since these expectations are based upon the preceding experience of the piece, and since the present state and configuration are mentally compared with whatever mental traces we have retained from previous states, each moment may be described as having a particular memory/expectancy valence. The way in which a particular piece creates and assembles memories of itself and the way in which it creates, assembles, confirms or denies expectancy may be considered its memory/expectancy structure. Recognition, which is also a kind of connection made through time, is, in this context, regarded as a form of memory.

In Chryssa's *Fragment for the Gates of Times Square, 2,* one sees a dark, almost opaque plastic box. Suddenly neon calligraphy flashes on inside, clearly visible because of its brilliance. After only three seconds, the light goes out, and the piece returns to its "inert," inscrutable state for 27 seconds before it lights up again. Thus two simple, disparate, motionless sculptural images are alternated in time to create a complex memory/expectancy structure. The first burst of light we see denies our impression that the piece is static and "timeless": we are surprised. But the period of illumination is much too short for us to study adequately the complex arrangement of neon in the contemplative manner we are accustomed to use with sculpture. The frustration intensifies our desire and anticipation. Each time the light goes on we continue our study, based on memories of the preceding "viewing periods." Each time the light goes out we ready ourselves for very pointed, accurate observation during the next illumination. As the piece is viewed over many repetitions, predictability of the durations in the fixed cycle becomes more accurate, the anticipatory tension becomes modified, and memory completes the perception of the briefly illuminated figure. The structure of the piece in time makes dynamic use of the memory/expectancy mode.

On the other hand, Robert Breer's work makes use of memory/expectancy in an entirely different way. While Chryssa's piece initially surprises us, almost all of its perceptual duration is involved with the fulfillment of expectancy. Although the effect is naturally more pronounced when many of Breer's small styrofoam floor pieces are seen together—as in his 1965 and 1967 shows at the Bonino Gallery where each work became merely part of a gallery-sized piece—even one of them has the ability to surprise through the denial and contradiction of the expectancies it creates. Unprepossessing in shape, devoid of detail, and painted a white that adds nothing to the visual interest, the piece hardly seems to move: in some of them, unseen wheels propel them so slowly that they do not appear to be in motion at all. The viewer is led to expect nothing and shifts his attention elsewhere. When he looks at the piece again, the object which appeared to be motionless is in a different spot; the piece traveling at a very slow rate has covered much more of the floor than was expected, and perhaps it has even changed direction (a mechanism inside reverses the wheels when the piece pushes against something). These effects depend primarily upon the fact that perceptual time tends to be judged according to the activity that fills it: an "empty" time seems long, a "busy" time seems short, etc. Of course no surprises occur with Breer's work if the piece is watched continually (in the "traditional" way) and no "different" time is interposed, but much of its esthetic power lies in its ability to create no expectancies, to ingratiate itself into a life situation, and to provide what is not expected.

It should be apparent that in discussing the memory/expectancy mode of perception, I am referring only to those memories and expectancies which give a particular "shape" to time. Of course any piece of kinetic sculpture creates basic and obvious expectancies (and memories) as to location, material, qualities, etc. We know very quickly that Chryssa's piece will not move, that Breer's pieces will not change color or light up, etc. These expectancies relating to the general nature of the piece are qualitative and formal rather than structural. They give the piece its over-all character rather than its durational uniqueness. (Just as Beethoven, and others, could write many works in the symphonic form, Thomas Wilfred, and others, can make lumia which are formally the same but structurally different.) In other words the memory/expectancy qualities that involve structure rather than form are, or become, dynamic. The memory of a quality is passive while that of an occurrence tends to be active. An expectancy that is denied becomes a structural element, while an expectancy must have a degree of uncertainty before it can structure the future, etc. In short, while the numerous psychological principles involving the dynamics of memory and expectancy cannot be investigated here, it can be said that every work exists in time, but not every work structures it. In this sense I believe that memory/expectancy is the only mode of perception in which we may say that a true structuring of time is involved. It is the mode most commonly operative in the traditional durational arts of music, drama, dance, etc., but it is not used in most kinetic sculpture. Although the other modes of kinetic experience partake of time, the same kind of "shape" through extended time is not realized.

If memory/expectancy is basically involved with time, we can find a type of experience of kinetics that, in contrast, stands almost outside of time. It could be called the static mode.

In December, 1966, at the Pace Gallery, two visitors were discussing Marjorie Strider's *Piece of Sea*. Bending over the blocky green polyester shape, the upper face of which was modeled to resemble ocean waves, they peered closely at the rivulets of water that lined the surface. One proposed that—in contradiction to the law of gravity, for the surface obviously sloped—the water was not moving. The other agreed—until it was demonstrated to them that the water could be diverted and change direction.

In Strider's piece, streams of water flow from small holes in the highest part, run slowly and smoothly down the face and sides, and are recirculated from an almost-invisible reservoir in the base. Light glints and shimmers from the surface of the water, but in many spots it is not easy to discern physical movement. This is not crucial to my point, however. Even when movement is easily apparent, there is no *change* in the movement. There is no point in comparing an observation at one moment with an observation at another moment. Memory and expectancy do not function dynamically. The piece is static. (Each time *Piece of Sea* is plugged in, the water takes a slightly different path. These "compositional" differences also do not matter. The piece is essentially unchanged.)

Thus in a static mode, kinesis creates a perceptual image that is not significantly different from a painted or sculpted one, although the quality of motion usually contributes a small share to the total experience. Static image sculpture of an entirely different sort than Strider's piece is the "virtual volume" work produced by the Bauhaus, Len Lye, etc.: a wire, plane, or solid of any kind is spun or rotated so rapidly that the observer sees a transparent and strangely immaterial "mass." Again movement is apparent. It is a quality of the image. But the image does not change with time. Memory/expectancy is not utilized, and a photograph, which registers the quality of motion, represents the experience with relative accuracy. (The exclusion of memory/expectancy would be possible, perhaps, if a comparison of the "on" and "off" states of the work was made an esthetic consideration, but the purpose here is to establish general concepts rather than to analyze any particular work in detail.)

233

The question "How long is the present moment?" is crucial for another mode in the experience of kinesis. Theoretically the present may be infinitely small or have no real duration. But in actuality the *feeling* of presence has some extension in time. Practically and operationally we can consider the present to have a certain shape and size. These functional limits of the present are indicated by two basic psychological experiments.

In the first experiment, the experimenter briefly shows the subject a number of marbles in a box or a number of dots on a card, etc. The duration of exposure is not long enough to allow the subject to *count* the number of units shown him, but he is asked to tell how many there are. Not surprisingly, answers are accurate in the low numbers and decrease in accuracy as the total of marbles, dots, or whatever, increases. The number of items which the subject can estimate correctly without counting is known as the "apprehension span": it is usually about four to six units, depending upon the type of unit, if no errors are allowed. With larger numbers the subject usually will not even attempt any kind of specific response, saying "There are about 35," etc.

The second experiment is immediate digit memory, which is a part of most intelligence tests. Number sequences of increasing length are presented to the subject, and, with no delay between presentation and response, he is asked to repeat them accurately. The average college student can usually repeat sequences up to eight digits.

These two experiments can be seen as representing the amplitude and duration, so to speak, of the present moment. A "vertical" limit on the simultaneous amount of material apprehended is indicated by the former experiment, and a "horizontal" limit on continuity and sequence is emphasized by the latter. Within these limits a certain type of memory and expectancy probably exist, but I prefer to use those terms for connections across "empty" intervals of the past and future. Rather than to differentiate between "continuous" and "discontinuous" memory, for example, it is best to use the word "memory" only as we have previously and to stress the wholistic character of the present moment.

Since the present moment has a certain amplitude, the experience of a kinetic work may exist entirely within its limits and yet not, of necessity, be static. In contrast to the static mode, it develops and changes. In contrast to the memory/expectancy mode, it is perceived totally without any extended dynamic claims to the past or future. Thus *Bascule* by Jean Tinguely, for example, rocks back and forth on a large curved metal plate while the belt-drive from its visible and organic motor turns a wheel which thrusts a bell-tipped metal rod out into space. Where in the static mode we had an image with the quality of motion, we now have a complete, sequential motion image that makes no claims on memory or expectation.

By referring to the concepts of memory/expectancy and of the present moment, we find that another mode of perception exists somewhat between the two. Naturally, as the perceptions of the present moment move into the past, they disappear: the complete, wholistic present can be "stretched" only so far. This disappearance is accelerated if new stimuli are presented rather than a neutral sensory field. In some cases, of course, elements of the present moment function as memories and create expectancies in the manner already discussed, but the point is that this creation of significant, functional memory does not necessarily happen. No matter how interesting the details of the present moment are, they may be completely unavailable to memory in a very short time.

Thus we have what perhaps could be called the "transitional mode" of kinetic perception, in which a series of different present moments flow one-into-the-other without creating operative memories or expectancies.

In the lumia works of Thomas Wilfred and his imitators, light is reflected onto the rear of a translucent screen, creating an abstract "painting" that is constantly changing. During each present moment we are aware of the type and direction of changes in color and form; of the character of the appearing, expanding, contracting, disappearing shapes; of the tempo or "pace" of the composition. A comparison might be made between a new image and one that has just faded away, but, as in digit memory, the mind can only hold the complete details of the sequence for a short time. It is not the esthetic purpose of most lumia to implant their complete sequence in memory. (A Museum of Modern Art press release of 1964 describing the newly-acquired *Lumia Suite, Op. 158* states, "The duration of the entire composition has not yet been calculated, but the length of other lumia compositions by Wilfred ranges from a few hours to more than 5,000 years.") Whether the imagery itself actually flows or is presented as a series of motionless configurations, etc., we have in the transitional mode a flow of present moments that do not attempt to hook up with the past or future.

In using lumia as our example, we must note that the form is not necessarily involved with the transitional mode. If we are told or assume that the structure is cyclical, expectancy may be operative as we search for the repetitions. If a form or color cycle is short, we may recognize it when it begins for the second or third time. With longer cycles, however, it is problematical how many repetitions would be necessary before memory/expectancy became involved, and since "beginning" and "end" are arbitrary, the usual mode involves a "wash" of various present moments which totally replace each other.

Although Harold Rosenberg (in *Vogue*, Feb. 1, 1967) states that the contemporary esthetic concern with motion "marks the end of contemplation," the transitional mode in particular can be seen as a contemplative one. As illustrated by Wilfred's lumia (or by "psychedelic" light shows) the ever-changing present contains too much detail to be completely apprehended, and past and future cease to exist: the "timelessness" of traditional contemplation is obtained in a different way. And since, on the other hand, the static mode is as "present" as a painting and no details are added or taken away by time, its contemplative possibilities would not seem to differ from the traditional ones.

Thus we have four modes in the perception of kinetic sculpture: the static, the present moment (or motion image), the transitional, and memory/expectancy. The important thing is that each is fundamentally unlike the others. Each has its own psychic territory, its own way of functioning. Investigation of the subtleties and nuances of these modes can only tell us more about art in general, because, in a very basic way, the experience is the work of art.

Index